D1294404

BRAVE NEW CITY

BRAVE NEW CITY

Brighton & Hove
Past, Present, Future

Anthony Seldon

with Matthew Nurse,
Edward Twohig and Chris Horlock

This book is dedicated to the memory of my dear Auntie Bess,
who loved Brighton and Hove, and who introduced me to it in the 1960s

First published in 2002 by Pomegranate Press, Dolphin House, 51 St Nicholas Lane, Lewes, Sussex BN7 2JZ
Email:sussexbooks@aol.com

© Text Anthony Seldon, 2002
Anthony Seldon reserves the moral right to be identified as the author of this work
The author is donating all his profits from this book to the Martlets Hospice, Hove

Principal researcher: Matthew Nurse

New photography © Edward Twohig
Archive photography: Chris Horlock
Architectural concepts © AROS
(Additional picture credits, page 156)

Book design: David Arscott at Pomegranate Press
Jacket design: Alan Wares at Medialab, Brighton
Cover imagery and Chapter 8 graphics by AROS

Inside front cover: the Carden Plan, from the Corporation's 1935 jubilee brochure
Inside back cover: the Seldon Plan, painted by Victoria Jones, June 2002

All rights reserved. No part of this publication may be reproduced, stored in a retrieval system
or transmitted in any form or by any means without the prior written permission of the copyright owner

By the same author:
Churchill's Indian Summer (1981); *By Word of Mouth* (with Joanna Seldon, 1983);
Contemporary History (ed., 1987); *Ruling Performance* (with Peter Hennessy, 1987);
Political Parties Since 1945 (ed., 1988); *The Thatcher Effect* (ed. with Dennis Kavanagh, 1989)
Politics UK (joint author, 1991); *The Conservative Century* (ed., 1994);
The Major Effect (ed. with Dennis Kavanagh, 1994); *The Heath Government 1970–74* (ed. with
Stuart Ball, 1996); *The Contemporary History Handbook* (ed. with Brian Brivati, 1996);
The Ideas that Shaped Post-war Britain (ed. with David Marquand, 1996);
How Tory Governments Fall (ed., 1996); *Major: a Political Biography* (1997);
The Thatcher Government 1979–90 (with Daniel Collings, 1998); *10 Downing Street: An Illustrated History* (1999);
The Powers Behind the Prime Minister (with Dennis Kavanagh, 1999); *The Foreign Office: An Illustrated History*
(2000); *The Blair Effect 1997–2001* (ed., 2001); *A New Conservative Century?* (with Peter Snowdon, 2001); *Public
and Private Education: The Divide Must End* (2001); *The Opening of the British Mind* (2002)

For news of a wide variety of Sussex titles contact the Sussex Book Club:
51 St Nicholas Lane, Lewes, Sussex BN7 2JZ; e-mail: sussexbooks@aol.com
Membership is free, there is no obligation to buy, and all books ordered are delivered free of p&p

ISBN: 0-9542587-1-1

British Library Cataloguing-in-Publication Data.
A catalogue record for this book is available from the British Library

Colour origination and printing by Viscan Graphics, Mimosa Road, Singapore

This book was supported by British Bookshops and Sussex Stationers

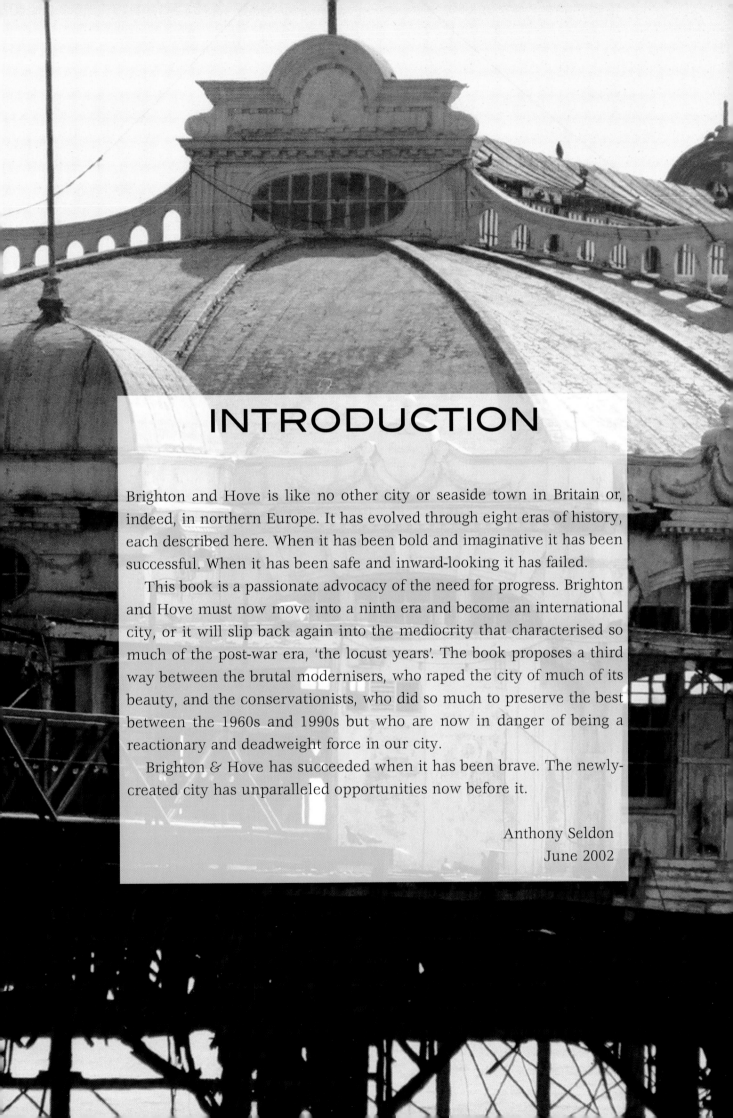

INTRODUCTION

Brighton and Hove is like no other city or seaside town in Britain or, indeed, in northern Europe. It has evolved through eight eras of history, each described here. When it has been bold and imaginative it has been successful. When it has been safe and inward-looking it has failed.

This book is a passionate advocacy of the need for progress. Brighton and Hove must now move into a ninth era and become an international city, or it will slip back again into the mediocrity that characterised so much of the post-war era, 'the locust years'. The book proposes a third way between the brutal modernisers, who raped the city of much of its beauty, and the conservationists, who did so much to preserve the best between the 1960s and 1990s but who are now in danger of being a reactionary and deadweight force in our city.

Brighton & Hove has succeeded when it has been brave. The newly-created city has unparalleled opportunities now before it.

Anthony Seldon
June 2002

BRIGHTON

For Health & Pleasure all the year round

THE FAMOUS SHELTERED WALK, MADEIRA DRIVE.

CONTENTS

IMAGES IN THIS SECTION
Facing page: Madeira Drive on 1930s poster
Frontispiece: The Palace Pier at night
Title page: Houses in the Steine

Facing title page: Brunswick Terrace
Introduction: The West Pier
Overleaf: Tallis map of Brighton c. 1855
Page 10: Tower blocks, lower Kemp Town

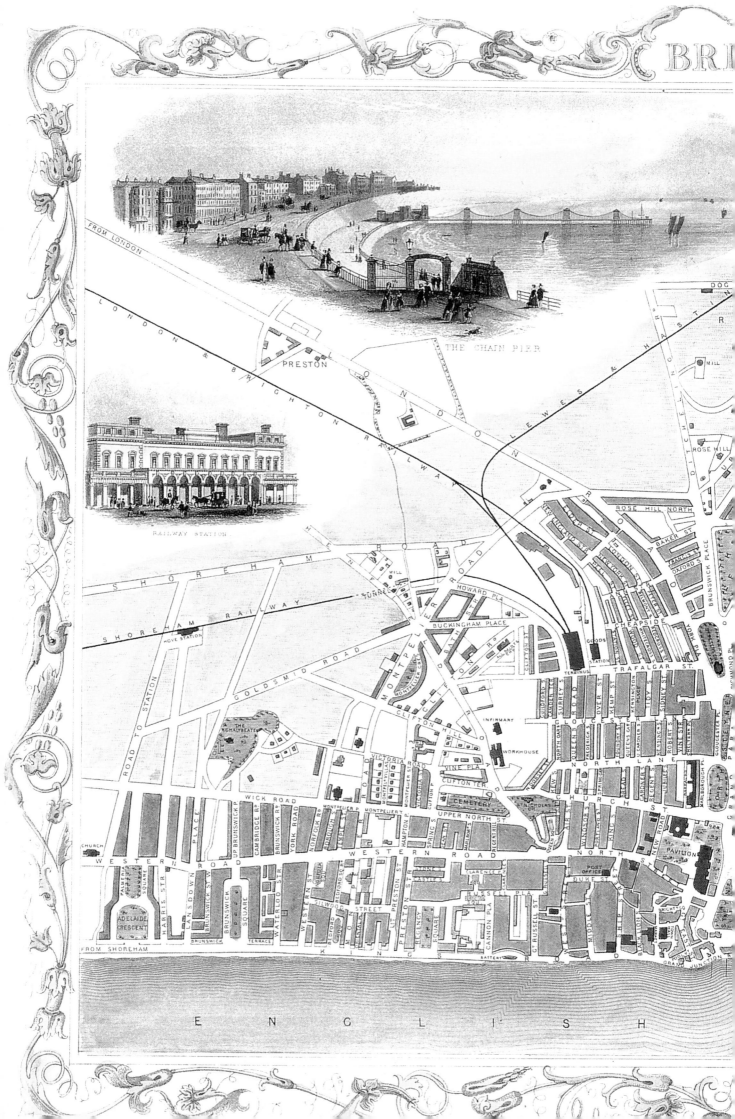

BRI

THE CHAIN PIER

RAILWAY STATION

ENGLISH

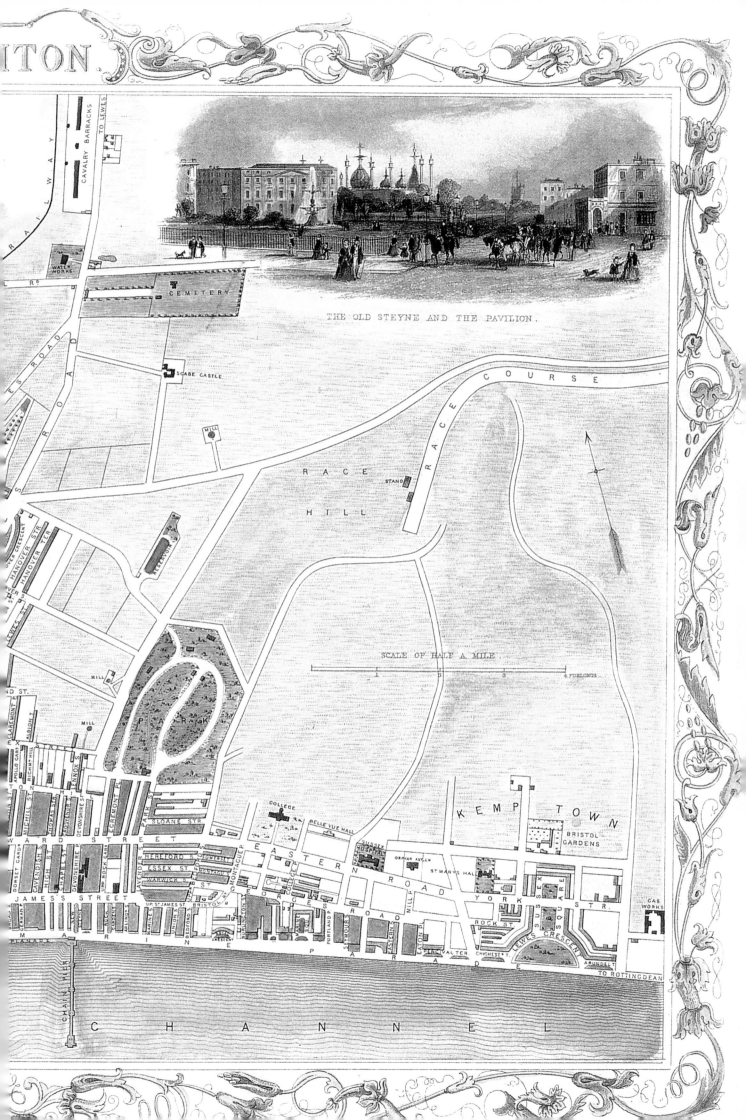

THE OLD STEYNE AND THE PAVILION.

ITON.

RAILWAY

CAVALRY BARRACKS

TO LEWES

TO LEWES

WATER WORKS

CEMETERY

ROAD

ROAD

SCABE CASTLE

MILL

RACE COURSE

RACE HILL

STAND

RESERVOIR

HANOVER CRESCENT

HANOVER STR

HANOVER TER

LEWES ST

SCALE OF HALF A MILE.

1   2   3   4 FURLONGS

MILL

MILL

PARK

COLLEGE

BELLE VUE HALL

KEMP TOWN

BRISTOL GARDENS

ND ST

CLAREMONT

ABBOTT

APOLLO GARD

RICHM.d HILL

SUSSEX HOSPITAL

ORPHAN ASYLUM

ST MARYS HALL

SLOANE STR

LENNOX

PARK ST

EGREMONT PL

HERTFORD S.t

MONTAGUE P.

COLLEGE

YORK

ROCK ST

GAS WORKS

MICHELL ST

THOMAS ST

HANOVER

DEVONSHIRE ST

EASTERN ROAD

HASTINGS.t

WARD STREET

DORSET GARD

CAVENDISH

HIGH ST

CHAPEL ST

UPP ROCK PLACE

AVENUE

ESSEX ST

WARWICK S.t

SUSSEX SQUARE

JAMES'S STREET

DEVONSHIRE ST

UP ST JAMES ST

BRISTOL S.t

BEDFORD

GEORGE S.t

COLLEGE

PORTLAND P.

EASTERN ROAD

MILL ST

ROCK ST

LEWES CRESCENT

CHICHEST.t T.

ARUNDEL T.

TO ROTTINGDEAN

CHAIN PIER

MARINE

PARADE

SEYMOUR S.t

EASTERN

P A R A D E

PERCIVAL T.R.

WALTER T.

CHANNEL

1
THE RAPE
OF THE CITY

Not all old buildings are sacred. Not all new buildings are second-rate. Towns are dynamic. The need for new transport, housing and working spaces means that old buildings that cannot be adapted have occasionally to make way for the new. These become testaments to the changing needs and aesthetic of the age and can sometimes outstrip in beauty those that they have replaced. It just so happens that in Brighton and Hove most of the eighteenth and nineteenth century buildings are beautiful (little survives from before 1750), while most of the twentieth century buildings are ugly, coarse and of no aesthetic value or interest.

Some older buildings and structures had to go, but the fact that so many buildings were destroyed in a town that could match any in the country, including Bath and Cheltenham, for the quality and elegance of its Georgian and Regency architecture, is a tragedy not just for Brighton and Hove but for the country. Future generations will demand to know the names of the barbarians, and the reasons why so many poor or ugly structures were put up in place of the beautiful or the historic.

This chapter highlights merely some of the worst of them.

COUNTDOWN TO HORROR
The city's worst architectural moments, in ascending order

12=

Black Rock Pool

Black Rock in east Brighton takes its name either from a large black rock, long since swept away, or from the fact that coal was once unloaded here. It is the point where the crumbling chalk of the South Downs meets the sea, and the site of the first desecration to be listed here – the first of many in a city which has seen many fine buildings and structures crumble to the ground.

To twentieth century Brightonians Black Rock is best known as the site of an outdoor swimming pool, opened in August 1936 with attractive changing rooms and a café. On its opening, the press commented that for some time there had been 'agitation in favour of the provision of an open-air bath on the same lines as those constructed in other well-known resorts,' and it warmly welcomed this 'magnificent open-air bath on the foreshore at Black Rock'.

Closed in 1978, it was subsequently demolished. With its destruction the city lost not only its last outdoor swimming pool (apart from Saltdean Lido), but an example of interwar marine architecture at its best.

Today the site is a haven for wall artists.

Demolished

The Black Rock swimming pool in 1939, with the eight-storey Marine Gate block of flats, almost completed, rising beyond it. As so often, one asks why something attractive and popular was pulled down without any benefit to local people whatsoever.

12=

Goldstone Football Ground

The Goldstone ground (previously Goldstone Farm) dates from September 1901. Brighton & Hove Albion moved to the ground in the 1902–3 season for their permanent home. The south stand was added in 1949, the west stand in 1958 and the north stand in 1984.

Like the nearby Sussex County Cricket Ground, the Goldstone was a valued part of the town's history, but it was sold for private profit in the 1990s and replaced by an unattractive set of retail warehouses. Council and local protest was swept aside. Even though the Albion needed a bigger ground than the Goldstone, it should not have been sold – especially as the city is in desperate need of sports grounds and stands.

The unlovely site at the top of the page was once home to Brighton & Hove Albion football club. The early photographs show (right) a full crowd at the Goldstone for a 1923 cup tie against Corinthians, and (below) hundreds of bicycles and a few cars parked for a home match c. 1910.

12=

Queen's Park
Attree Villa and German Spa

Originally called 'Brighton Park', this was laid out as a 'subscription' park (you paid for the right to use it) in 1824. Thomas Attree, a local solicitor, bought the land very soon afterwards and, inspired by London's Regent's Park, commissioned the distinguished architect Charles Barry to design two formal entrances and a series of Italianate villas in a semi-circle around the park. A painting of Barry's conception survives (*see p. 47*).

The first villa, one of the earliest in Britain in the Italianate style, was completed in 1830. Lived in by Attree himself, it had a shallow roof, broad eaves and a loggia of three round-headed glass windows. Despite being classed as an outstanding building by the Historic Buildings Council, this beautiful villa was demolished in 1971–72. All that remains of Barry's work is the gazebo and the 60ft high 'pepper pot' tower which was probably used as a water tank for the villa.

In 1836 Attree renamed the gardens 'Queen's Park' in honour of Queen Adelaide, wife of William IV (1830-37). At the southern end of the park stood another historic building, Struve's Royal German Spa (so named in 1835). All that remains is the Ionic portico and north wall (*p. 37*): the romantic structure behind has been destroyed, and with it was lost one of the few remaining links with the second period in Brighton's history, the Seaside Resort Era.

Below: Attree's villa in 1835, with the 'pepper pot' seen to the right of it.

Right: The tower today. Apart from the gazebo, it is all that survives of the villa today.

Demolished

11 Imperial Theatre

The 1,877-seat Imperial Theatre opened in North Street on the eve of the darkest days of the second world war (April 9, 1940) and was the last traditional theatre to be erected in Brighton. Its interior and foyer were in exquisite late Art Deco style, while its auditorium had fine detailing and was painted vermilion, pale jade and gold. The mayor, on its opening, described it with understandable local pride as 'England's most beautiful theatre'. Initially the Imperial presented drama and variety shows, but the wartime audiences wanted films, which it also offered from 1943. Between 1950 and 1964 it was the Essoldo Cinema; then a bingo hall; next a venue for a variety of different events; and latterly the Hot Shots entertainment centre.

Elegant in design, and centrally located, it was pulled down in 2001 to make way for 'new developments'. This building is selected because it shows that the demolition of historic and important buildings continues despite all the agitation from conservation groups. At the same time, monstrosities such as Gala Bingo in Eastern Road have been built, when the Imperial could have been used for this purpose – as it was in the past.

Right: A sorry sight. The building stands derelict in 1996, five years before it was demolished.

Below: Inside the Imperial Theatre on its opening night in 1940.

Gone – Imperial Theatre

10

King Street

Imagine an historic Brighton street named after George III, one of the first to be built beyond the confines of the old rectangular medieval town. Imagine houses and shops, some from the eighteenth century and some nineteenth, some flint-fronted and some brick, with a variety of Georgian and Victorian windows. Imagine, too, a public house, the Running Horse, as one of the street's focal points.

Then imagine many houses flattened and the street cut in half. Imagine a three-storey car park with an irregular brick and concrete frontage transecting the street. No, the top image on this page is not a trick photograph. Who has benefited from the change? Do the decision-makers, the planners and the National Car Park executives live in the street or nearby?

A street cut in half

King Street, between Church Street and North Street, 1964. It was later blocked off by a car park (top picture) and is now known as King Place.

9

Central National School

One of the earliest schools in a city that became known in the nineteenth century as 'School town' was the Central National School of 1829 in Church Street. Founded by Henry Wagner and built in Regency Gothic style, it boasted pinnacles and delightful oriel windows and dominated the view of Church Street when looked at from New Road. Later re-named the Central Voluntary Primary School, it closed in 1967.

A postal dispute and human error prevented receipt of the preservation order that would have prevented the corporation from demolishing it in 1971. A great treasure and work of art was lost.

What looks like a bomb site in Church Street, opposite New Road (above), was once graced by the Central National School. Note the hotel at the left of the old photograph. The site has remained empty for more than 30 years.

8

Hove Town Hall

Hove and Brighton were both blessed with fine nineteenth-century town halls. Brighton's was completed in 1831 to the designs of Thomas Cooper – planned in the pattern of a Greek cross, with two-storey porticoes on three of the four sides (although, in the event, only three of the four arms were to be built because of wrangles over the land). Criticised on its inception as 'designed after a day trip to Greece,' it is admittedly rather an overblown, though still an elegant, building.

Hove had the more distinguished town hall (*below*), built on Church Road in 1882 by Alfred Waterhouse, designer of the Metropole Hotel. Nikolaus Pevsner described it as 'red, Gothic, hard and imperishable'. There is little non-ecclesiastical Victorian Gothic in the city, and this was a fine example.

Brighton's original town hall still stands, but Hove's, burned to the ground in January, 1966, was replaced in 1974 by a concrete and glass building widely criticised for its unattractiveness and inappropriateness in its environment. Although a poorer building than the one it replaced, the new Hove town hall is not without merit, and it is likely to be more highly regarded in years to come.

Above: The original town hall at Hove, which was destroyed by fire. Facing page: Brighton's town hall (top right) was less distinguished than Hove's (right), but it easily wins the contest today – although in years to come the new Hove town hall is likely to be judged more generously.

'Buildings are three-dimensional works of art. Some of the most celebrated artists of their day once worked in Brighton and Hove, among them John Nash, Charles Barry, Decimus Burton, Robert Adam and George Gilbert Scott. If paintings or sculptures had been destroyed there would have been a national outcry. Why do we regard the works of architects differently?'

7 Kemp Town Railway Station

The Kemp Town branch line, just under two-and-a-half miles of track, was built in 1866–9 by the London, Brighton and South Coast Railway Company. Trains ran almost a mile along the line to Lewes and then branched off. Apart from the station building itself (very similar in style to the still-standing example at Hove), its two chief features were the graceful Lewes Road viaduct, carrying the track 50ft above Lewes Road and

Melbourne Street, and the Kemp Town tunnel, cut through the chalk and more than half a mile long.

Passenger trains were full at the peak, but competition from buses and cars led to a fall in demand, and the passenger service was terminated in 1932. The line was then used for goods traffic, and it became the Brighton East Goods Depot until, in 1971, dwindling business led to the remaining traffic being transferred to Hove.

Proposals were made by a group including Gavin Henderson (former artistic director of the Brighton Festival) to convert the Kemp Town buildings into a railway museum, with special steam trains running to it from Brighton Station. Exhibits were readily available, but nothing transpired. Different proposals were then made for the track's use as an urban walkway, but in the event the land was sold to a property developer.

Factories of drab uniformity have been erected on the site. The town needs industrial estates, but putting one in the middle of Kemp Town was a clear error: space could have been found for it on empty sites near the bypass, reducing heavy traffic into the centre of town. Most insulting of all is the profoundly ugly Gala Bingo Hall on the main Eastern Road, which boasts an ersatz steam

Cleared for development

train of uncertain design apparently emerging from a black tunnel. Presumably this is meant as an historical allusion. It is thoughtfully detailed and is in its way a touching emblem, but it is also in poor taste. The approach to the whole site along Eastern Road is a barren urban wilderness, devoid of plants, beauty and humanity.

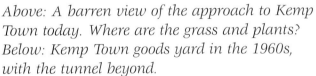

Above: A barren view of the approach to Kemp Town today. Where are the grass and plants?
Below: Kemp Town goods yard in the 1960s, with the tunnel beyond.
Left: Steam engine at the station, c. 1900.
Right: The Freshfield industrial estate taking shape in 1975.
Top right: Modern memorial on the bingo hall.

6

Palace Pier Theatre

The Palace Pier, much altered and now calling itself Brighton Pier, still stands. The building at its end does not. Opened just two years after the pier itself, it replicated the Royal Pavilion in style, with several minaret towers. In 1910–11 it was remodelled as perhaps the most beautiful theatre in the whole town.

'This book is not against change, nor is it for conservation at all costs. It is for progress. But the new buildings that progress brings must be beautiful – as beautiful in their own way as the finest historic buildings in the city.'

When the pier was taken over by new owners in 1984, they dismantled the theatre and constructed a funfair and amusements park in its place, pledging to replace it with a facsimile complete with colonnade, oriental domes and many of the original fittings. It had been for a time the official theatre of the Brighton Festival, and hopes ran high that it would be restored elsewhere to its former glory. All these years on, however, the theatre has not been reassembled. Parts of it lie rotting in a warehouse somewhere near Brighton.

Above: An act of vandalism. The graceful Palace Pier Theatre is demolished in 1984.

Below: The theatre in 1902.

Dismantled

5

Western Road/ 'old' Churchill Square

Not originally in the old town, Western Road came into being in the early nineteenth century as a track through fields linking North Street with the newly emerging Brunswick Town. Named after the property-owning Western family of Preston Manor (although also happily indicating the road's direction), it was already lined with large houses in the 1830s, and by the 1860s some were converted into shops.

Road widening, mostly in the 1920s and 1930s, dictated that many of these buildings were lost, to be replaced by unimaginative, generally unattractive interwar stores. The birthplace of the inventor Magnus Volk was one of a handful of 1820s listed buildings which managed to survive, some with bowfronts and some faced with glazed 'mathematical tiles'.

The worst excrescence was named after Winston Churchill, who attended a prep school in Hove, briefly and unhappily. In 1959 Brighton Council decided to develop Western Road on the south side where it adjoined North Street. In the philistine early 1960s, when the Conservative government gave their assent to the destruction of so many fine buildings, permission was readily granted for the council to clear a 15-acre site from Western Road down to King's Road on the seafront. (The King's Road despoilations are listed in this chapter as the No. 1 desecration.)

The shopping centre, Churchill Square, was built between 1965 and 1972. Hauntingly ugly, it was perhaps best exemplified by a concrete sculpture 'the Spirit of Brighton' (*below and on p. 11*), which stood in front of Chartwell Court – named after Churchill's country residence. The old man would not have been amused, but might have thought the statue an apt comment on the spiritual depth of the town's decision-makers.

With his highly developed artist's sense, Churchill would probably have found the redeveloped Churchill Square, opened in the late 1990s, far more pleasing.

Unlamented eyesore

The original Churchill Square in a derelict state, June 1991, with the extraordinary 'Spirit of Brighton' sculpture on the right.

4

Lower Kemp Town

The damage here was not to seafront Kemp Town, which has been largely preserved and is the finest unbroken line of Regency architecture in Britain: the concern here is the streets behind.

Some of these houses were erected in the 1820s and 1830s, some later in the century. They included slums which, dank and run-down though they were, could have been modernised in the way that similar housing stock has been in other towns. Instead, row after row of houses was flattened.

Destruction began in the 1930s, although the inhabitants then were given new homes in estates with real houses, in Moulescomb and elsewhere. After the war it was different: tower block flats were erected for the former 'slum' dwellers. These towers now dominate the skyline, with Theobald House (the tallest council flats in Brighton) rising to 19 storeys. Opened to acclaim in 1966, it boasted 110 modern flats with all conveniences. Did anyone ask the inhabitants whether they would sooner live renovated houses with front doors, character and their own gardens?

Ancient streets were not all that was swept away, with their communities ripped apart: shops and meeting places were also destroyed. Is this progress?

Flattened

Above: These shops in Upper St James's Street were destroyed in the 1970s and replaced with the unsightly blocks in the top picture. A mark of progress?

Left: a penthouse view from the new Theobald House in September, 1966.

A view of Queen's Road in 1866, looking south with the sea in the distance.

3 Queen's Road, east side

Queen's Road was built as a direct consequence of the railway opening in 1841. It ran due south, straight down the hill from the station and joining the corner of the old town, where West Street met North Street. Today it remains the principal thoroughfare for visitors arriving in the city by train.

Constructed in 1845, the road soon became lined with shops and houses, hotels and public houses. It was widened in 1878, mainly at the railway company's expense,

The route from the railway station to the sea is now a depressing vista.

and so avoided suffering from the brutal road-widening programmes of the 1920s and 1930s. This makes it all the more incredible that so many buildings on the east side of the road should have been knocked down, with ugly office buildings erected in their place.

Queen's Road had been the centre of the town's medical profession in the late nineteenth century, and the eastern side had many fine dispensaries, such as the Brighton Hove and Preston Provident Dispensary (now Queensbury House). Two of the worst losses were Oddfellows Hall, built in 1854 and replaced by a nondescript office block, and the Regent Cinema, Britain's first super-cinema when it opened in 1921. The cinema and a bank next to it have been replaced by the ugly Boots store of 1979.

One's faith in the judgement of the town's planners is not improved by the preservation and renovation of the Clock Tower opposite Boots – donated by a benefactor in order to commemorate Queen Victoria's golden jubilee in 1887, and described by Pevsner as 'worthless'. The mediocre remains: the finery is destroyed. Victoria did little for the town beyond leaving it this eyesore.

25

2 The Bedford Hotel

The Bedford Hotel was opened in October 1829, designed by Thomas Cooper, architect of Brighton town hall. The Bedford was by far the finer building of the two – better proportioned and fitting more comfortably into its environment. After the Royal Pavilion, it was regarded as perhaps the finest Regency building in the town. Standing five storeys high, it had recessed frontages facing south and west, with two recessed Ionic porticoes. The doorway opened on to an entrance hall, with more Ionic columns and a glazed dome reminiscent of Barry's Reform Club in Pall Mall.

By mid-century it had established itself not only as Brighton's leading hotel, but also as one of the most luxurious in the south of

Burned down

The original Bedford Hotel, photographed c. 1880 and (top) in flames on April 4, 1964.

England. The first choice of royalty and the fashionable, its guests included Charles Dickens, who wrote part of *Dombey and Son* while staying there. The book's Major Bagstock, wanting urgently to make the acquaintance of Mr Dombey, effects his wish by travelling to Brighton. Dickens' biographer Peter Ackroyd relates that the writer came here to work on the book, welcoming the place for its 'peace and sea air'.

Although the building of the Grand Hotel (1864) and the Metropole (1890) challenged the Bedford's primacy, it continued to trade well on its glamorous image. In the early 1960s, however, its then owners sought permission to pull it down and replace it with a 14-storey block. Fierce objections were raised, but it burned down on April 1, 1964: there seem to have been a quite a lot of fires in Brighton and Hove in these years. Allegations of arson were made, given added piquancy by the fact that lives were lost in the fire.

The Bedford merits its high ranking in this list because a particularly fine seaside building was lost, to be replaced by an irredeemably grim building now called the Hilton West Pier – one of the ugliest in the city, and vastly damaging to the precious integrity of the seafront.

It is well worth examining this building, which, when it opened in 1967, was the first major new hotel development in the town for more than half a century. What a wasted opportunity! Did the architects think they were designing something of elegance? Where was their aesthetic sense? It will be hard to find a starker contrast anywhere of the beautiful being replaced by the gross.

A thing of beauty is a joy for ever. The Bedford Hotel has been replaced on the seafront by one of the ugliest buildings in the city.

1

Kingswest/ Conference Centre/ West Street

Occasionally one encounters something in life so utterly atrocious that it can be a valuable experience. It is the opposite experience of encountering an object or moment of incomparable beauty. The world suddenly seems to slot better into place, one's sense of value clarified.

The great virtue of Kingswest is its very awfulness. It would be difficult to conceive any building more lacking in merit or appropriateness to its environment. If one held an architectural competition, for gifted as well as poor architects, and asked them to design a deplorable building by the seafront, it is hard to imagine that they could have dreamt up anything like this. It is truly one of the worst buildings in Britain.

Put it alongside the grim Conference Centre and the modernised West Street, all of which entailed destroying a network of small streets and old houses, public houses and church buildings (the Grand Hotel itself only narrowly survived), and it is abundantly clear that there could be no more apt candidate than this for the city's worst desecration.

The buildings fronting West Street, King's Road and Kent Street were demolished in 1963. The Kingswest structure, initially with no windows but a crown of aluminium diamond shapes designed to 'glitter in the sun',

The Kingswest site in about 1930. The West Pier is in the background.

The Brighton Centre (left) and Kingswest sandwiched between elegant 19th century buildings.

was opened in 1965. The building never knew what it was. Neither did the public. It metamorphosed from dance hall to conference hall to ice-rink to bowling alley to cinema. A cinema with a sea view! The conference centre was differently ugly, but was like Kingswest in that it also showed no sensitivity to its location.

Historic West Street has gone. A guide book by Harold P. Clunn, published in 1925, captures the importance and glamour of West Street to Brighton:

'Every great metropolis has its world-famed streets which are the pride and glory of its citizens...Of such are Piccadilly and Regent Street in London, the grand boulevards and the Rue de La Paix in Paris,

Fifth Avenue in New York and West Street...the leading thoroughfare of this town of Brighton.'

Saddest of all for the town are the disappearances of the buildings and vistas, of the history and spirit. If the replacements had understood their environment, then the loss would have been ameliorated. But instead, one has a leisure complex that by its very nature does not need to have seaviews and a conference centre that has quickly become unsuitable for its task, built in a bleak and soulless environment which is a magnet for litter and vandalism.

Kingswest and the Conference Centre must go. Soon. But the old buildings and the history have been lost for ever.

2
THE GLORIOUS 18TH AND 19TH CENTURIES

Largely ignored by the Romans, lacking a natural harbour and situated equidistant between two river mouths (the Adur and the Ouse); not deemed worthy of a medieval castle or seen as suitable for a naval base; not sitting on top of a fertile mineral source or other natural resource; not blessed by gentle, sandy beaches – this was a great, if very peculiar, location for what developed into Britain's premier seaside town.

By 1900 much of the building that makes Brighton and Hove the beautiful city it is today had been erected. The glorious two-and-a-half-mile white-cream seafront from Sussex Square in east Brighton to Adelaide Crescent in Hove, the piers and many of the fine buildings behind the seafront were already in place. By 1900, Brighton was indisputably the most popular and successful seaside and holiday town in Britain.

The eighteenth and nineteenth were two glamorous centuries for Brighton and Hove, and during these years five distinct phases of history can be defined.

The Fishing Era: Saxons to 1730s

Brighton, originally named Brighthelmstone, was a seaside community many years before the Norman Conquest of 1066. The derivation of the name (which has many differing legitimate spellings) is as hazy as the precise origin of the town. The probable root is from a Saxon personal name, and 'tun', homestead. The Saxons would indeed appear to have been the first people permanently to settle in the area. The reason is unknown, but it may have because it was the point where the chalky Downs ended in the sea, and where there was an extensive beach protected from the full force of the English Channel by a submerged bar of shingle. A small inlet into the Steine may also have existed, long since destroyed by erosion.

The Domesday Book of 1086 records Brighthelmstone as consisting of 18 villagers, 9 smallholders with three ploughs and one slave. After the Norman era it slowly evolved as a fishing and farming community of some significance. A town constable was appointed in 1285, a market charter was granted in 1313 by Edward II, and the parish church of St Nicholas (*facing page*) was constructed. The first drawing of the town, probably an illustration of the attack by the French in

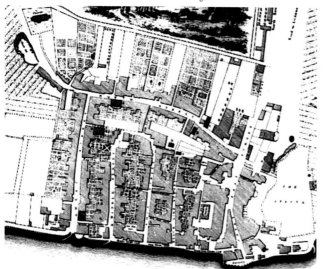

An early map of Brighton, showing the old town lying between West, North and East streets, with very little development beyond.

1514 when the town was burned, shows the main town in a rectangle bounded by the sea and by West, North and East streets.

On the east side of what became known as the 'old town' was an open area, used by fishermen for working on their nets, and subsequently called 'the Steine' after the Scandinavian word 'staene' (a place of stones) as it was the channel for the Wellsbourne stream, which now flows into the sea underground. Dwellings also extended to the east of the Steine, with a few fishermen's cottages sheltering under the cliffs (now Madeira Drive). Surrounding the rectangular old town was a large network of five fields, called 'laines', each of which was subdivided into strips. The North Laine was situated where the community of that name stands today, the streets still following the routes of the former thoroughfares across it.

Because the French burned the town in 1514, little of medieval Brighton remains, St Nicholas church being the chief exception. It is clearly seen on the first drawings of the town, on raised ground just outside the old town. An earlier church on the same site is recorded in the Domesday Book.

Recovery was swift after the 1514 trauma. The town flourished under Henry VIII (1509–47) and later Tudor monarchs. The town's prosperity swelled on the back of a fishing fleet landing cod and herring in the far away North Sea. Boats sailed off during the months of September and October, later calling in at Newcastle to buy coal with the profits from fish sold in Yarmouth, Scarborough and other ports. By 1600 the town boasted 80 fishing boats, employing some 400 fishermen and using 10,000 nets.

The town was made more secure with the building of a blockhouse, a circular fort on the cliffs (long since reclaimed by pounding seas), as well as a town wall. A local body called 'the twelve' was set up after 1580 to oversee the community's law and order.

Between 1550 and 1650 the population rose four-fold to about 4,000. Mackerel fishing was introduced in the second half of the sixteenth century. By the time that Charles I lost his head in 1649, Brighton was the largest, most important town in Sussex. His son, later Charles II, was Brighton's first royal visitor: in 1651 he stayed overnight at the George Inn in West Street (it was renamed the King's Head in his honour) before fleeing to France.

Fortunes were to dip in the second half of the seventeenth century, with Brighton's fishing industry going into decline. Smaller catches, sporadic attacks from the Dutch and French, storm damage to sea groynes and to houses (notably in the great storm of 1665), and the erosion of the cliffs and beach, all took their toll. Some local boats moved west to the Adur estuary at Shoreham, while others ceased to trade. By the 1680s a mere 30 vessels remained, and in 1697 only four sailed around the coast of Kent to Yarmouth. Cargo trade offered some relief, but many fishermen drifted off to London or to the east coast of England.

The year 1688 might have seen a 'glorious revolution' for the country at large, with William III peacefully succeeding James II as monarch, but there was nothing glorious about Brighton in this period. It was a forlorn town dedidedly down on its luck, with a falling and economically reduced population.

This state of affairs, however, was very soon to change.

Above: St Nicholas was built during the 14th century.

Left: Fishermen on Brighton Beach, 1871. The fishing industry has always been important to Brighton and Hove.

Page 30: Early 19th century houses overlooking Victoria Gardens in the Steine.

Page 31: The railway station with its beautiful glass roof.

Three Grand Houses . . .

lie well beyond the historic old town, all of them with important histories.

The oldest is **Patcham Place**, one of the first sights to greet those arriving in Brighton from the north by car. Originally built in the year of Elizabeth I's accession, 1558, its frontage was altered in 1764, giving it an eighteenth century appearance. The black mathematical tiles, which are hung from a wooden frame, can be seen deployed elsewhere in Brighton – notably in Royal Crescent.

One of Patcham Place's owners, Anthony Stapley, was a signatory to Charles I's death warrant. Another, Major Paine, had the foresight in 1840 to insist that the London–Brighton railway pass his land hidden in a tunnel.

Patcham Place was acquired by Brighton Corporation in 1937, and is currently used as a youth hostel.

Midway between Patcham place and the old town, **Preston Manor** stands on the site of a building which dates back to the late sixteenth century. In 1738 the lord of the manor, Thomas Western, ordered it to be rebuilt, and most of what already existed was destroyed.

In 1794 the house and some 400 hectares were bought by William Stanford. The future development of Hove became possible when the family eventually began selling the land, which stretched from the seafront beyond west Brighton back to Ditchling Road. Preston Park was created from land sold to the town in 1883.

In 1905 the family appointed Charles Stanley Peach to remodel the building and add an extra wing, creating the Edwardian house we see today. After 1933, when ownership of the house passed to the town, it was opened to the public as a museum, celebrating life 'below stairs' as well as the relatively sumptuous conditions above.

Patcham Place is well over four centuries old.

Stanmer House is the furthest removed geographically from the old town, being three miles from the Steine towards Lewes. An older manor house once stood on the site, and parts of it were incorporated in the rear of the current house when the French architect Nicholas Dubois designed it in the Palladian style in 1721. It has a fine rococo interior. The owners, the Pelhams, later extended it, destroying its symmetry.

The Pelhams gradually acquired land to the north-east of Brighton, but by 1880 they were forced to begin selling it off. In 1947 Brighton Corporation bought the remaining land, demolishing the house's delapidated west wing but preserving Stanmer Park for public enjoyment and providing the land on which Sussex University was built.

Stanmer House was renovated in 1961 when it became the administrative headquarters of the University of Sussex, but it later fell into disrepair, and it entered the twenty–first century with argument raging about how best to preserve it.

Stanmer House (above) and Preston Manor (top).

The Seaside Resort Era: 1730s–1780s

Brighton has often been down at heel. The early eighteenth century saw part of the cliffs flaking off into the sea and the market moving back from the shore to Black Lion Street in the heart of the rectangular old town. In 1700 the town's justices applied for poor relief. Brighton was palpably depressed.

A fresh start came from an improbable source, a doctor in Lewes who wrote *A Dissertation on the Use of Seawater in Diseases of the Glands*. Dr Richard Russell has been described as 'the undisputed founder of modern Brighton'. From the 1740s he began to send his patients here for a 'sea-water cure'. So successful did it prove that Russell decided to move his medical practice to Brighton – at the south end of the Steine, where the Royal Albion Hotel now stands.

Important though Russell was, however, one can exaggerate his claim to be the saviour of Brighton, because the town was already developing as a seaside resort from the 1730s, when seabathing visitors began to arrive – not least because Brighton provided a cheaper alternative to rapidly developing inland spas like Tunbridge Wells and Bath.

The Pelham family of Stanmer House (*p. 35*) bathed in the sea at Brighton from the 1750s. It was becoming a fashionable pastime in the early eighteenth century, with Hastings and Margate two other towns to flourish under the vogue.

Brighton was to develop rapidly in this spa resort era, and it took over from Scarborough as Britain's most popular seaside resort. The process was helped greatly, then as since, by its being the closest south coast town to London. During these years road transport from the capital improved markedly, the journey by coach being reduced from eight to as little as four or five hours, with macadamised roads making for much smoother journeys.

From 1760 the town also became a popular route to the continent, passengers boarding the cross-channel boats from the beach: a perilous means, one might think. Investment flooded in, much of it into the old town area, creating hotels, bathing facilities and libraries. The sea had now come to be viewed, not as a necessary convenience for trade, but as a source of recreation and

Dr Richard Russell's house in 1786. The Royal Albion Hotel would later be built on the site.

vitality. Bathing machines were a frequent sight on the beach during the season.

Health continued to be a cornerstone of the town long after Russell's death in 1759. Anthony Relhan, a fellow doctor, was recommending both immersion in as well as (incredibly) the drinking of sea-water as vital health-giving forces. Bottled Brighton sea water came to be advertised and sold in London: there is, alas, no record as to its effectiveness. More valuably, Relhan also promoted relaxation and the inhalation of sea air as restorative. Another physician, John Awsiter, recommended indoor bathing, which sparked off the building of covered baths, and a boost to the town's popularity even in inclement weather. Indoor bathing also compensated for the pebbled beaches and steep shelving that has always characterised Brighton's beaches, making them uncomfortable and even hazardous for bathing in contrast to the gentler beaches at Worthing. Baths first built on the beach in 1768 would later become part of Pool Valley. These baths were greatly enlarged by George Gilbert Scott in 1869 and survived until 1929 when the Savoy Theatre was put on the site.

Sea-bathing remained popular, despite the cold and the inhospitable beaches. Immersion before breakfast was encouraged. The well-off would undress in a bathing machine, which was manoeuvred by horse into the shallow waters. Men then bathed generally naked, women wearing a sack-like garment. More expensive bathing machines had screens to prevent the swimmers being viewed from the shore by telescope.

A German physician, Frederick Struve, was another to continue the health tradition, establishing the Royal German Spa at the south end of Queen's Park in the 1820s. Struve imitated and sold famous German mineral waters

The remains of Dr Struve's Royal German Spa in Queen's Park.

from places such as Ems and Marienbad. Visitors flocked to East Brighton from eight in the morning to take the waters. The 1820s also saw the publication of Sake Deen Mahomed's popular handbook *Shampooing* (which meant massaging). Many years before, this enterprising Indian had established Mahomed's Warm, Cold and Vapour Baths on a site which is now Queen's Hotel on the seafront.

Mahomed was one of several Brightonians originally from overseas whose zest and ingenuity contributed hugely to the town's development. His practice benefited from the recommendation of none other than Dr John Gibney, senior physician at the Royal Sussex County Hospital, which opened in 1828 to Charles Barry's designs on its present site in Kemp Town.

The sea water cure. Early facilities on the beach at Brighton.

37

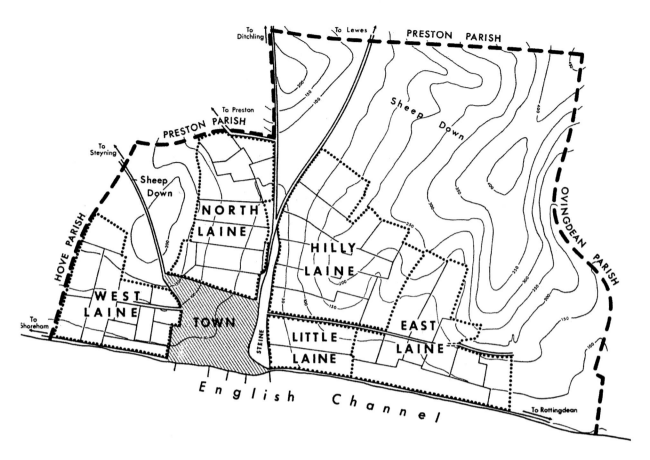

These two maps show the rapid growth of the town during the Seaside Resort and the Royal and Regency eras. In around 1740 (above) the old town still lay between East, West and North streets and the sea, with farmland (divided into 'laines') all around it. By 1831 (below) the population had risen from about 2,000 to some 40,000. The old town is picked out in red.

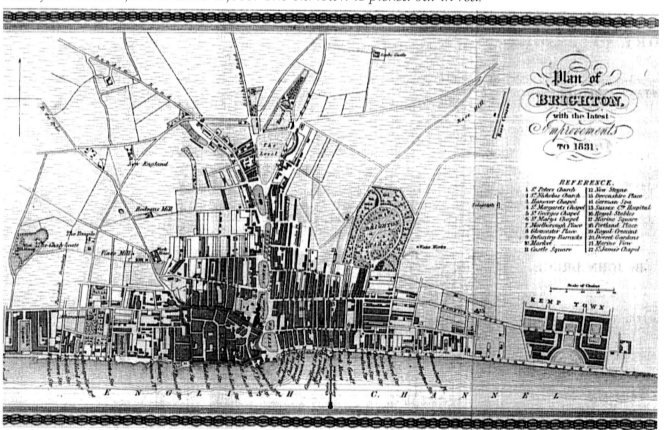

The Royal and Regency Era: 1770s–1830s

Our third era was ushered in by the visit in September 1783 of George, Prince of Wales and eldest son of George III. 'Prinnie', who was to become Prince Regent in 1811, arrived in a town already established as the country's most fashionable seaside resort and with Bath the only spa resort to rival it. But it still had a population of only 4,000, confined largely to the old rectangular town. By 1840, however, the population had grown tenfold to some 46,000, and the town had spread in all directions back from the sea.

Census figures reveal the 1820s to have been the most significant decade for population growth, from 25,000 to 40,000. Dwellings sprung up in the large farmland areas of the five laines: North, West, Hilly, East and Little Laine. Much of the new building was in the form of fashionable Regency terraces along the seafront with allied cheaper dwellings behind.

The old town developed into the commercial and the resort centre, and became the arrival and departure point for coaches: in 1822, as many as 62 horse-drawn coaches left Castle Square every day bound for London and elsewhere. King's Road, built by public subscription along the seafront, was opened by George IV (as the Prince Regent had by now become) in 1822. Regency and Bedford Squares were built to the west of the old town, Royal Crescent to the east (between 1798 and 1807) and the great Lewes Crescent and Sussex Square (*right*) further east still. Queen's Park was begun to the north-east.

Even before the Prince's first visit the place had royal connections. George's 1783 visit was to his uncle, the Duke of Gloucester, who had himself first come to the town in 1765, and the town was already developing genteel attractions, including ballrooms – the Castle had opened its ballroom in the early 1750s. But it was the Prince's enthusiasm for Brighton which was to transform the town. He decided to build a seaside residence in order to be near Maria Fitzherbert, his newly wedded wife. (The next few pages cover the history of the Pavilion and Dome.)

In 1793, instructions were given for a church to be built on North Street, on the boundary of the old town. Completed in 1795, it was intended to serve as an overflow for the overcrowded St Nicholas, still the only Anglican church for the town. The vicar hoped to attract the Prince to his new church, the Chapel Royal. But George was an irregular congregant, and never returned after a sermon on morality upset him.

Continued on page 44

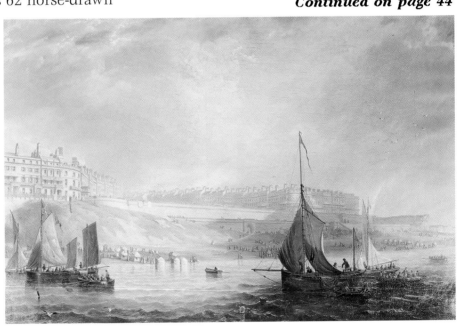

John Wilson Carmichael: 'Kemp Town from the Sea'.

The Royal Pavilion . . .

is not only Brighton's best known building: it is also one of the most recognisable in the country.

The Prince of Wales (later George IV) fell in love with Brighton following his first visits to the town in 1783 and 1784. In 1786 he employed Henry Holland to build him a permanent house on the site of an existing farmhouse on the west side of the Steine. The building, called the Marine Pavilion, was a two-storey villa in the shape of a letter 'E', with a domed rotunda and six Ionic columns at the centre, a domed saloon behind and bowed wings on either side. The original interiors were in a flamboyant French-inspired style.

In 1802 the Prince was reputedly presented with some Chinese wallpaper, and he was so struck by the style that he ordered the whole of his new house to be decorated in Chinese style. The following year he also required capacious horse stables, and William Porden built these for him under a huge dome, plus a riding school to the design of the Paris Corn Market. The stable could accommodate 44 horses, with grooms' quarters in the circular galleries. The dome itself (now the Brighton Dome), 80 feet in diameter and 60 feet high, was one of the largest in the world when it was finished in 1805. The riding school (the Corn Exchange), built in 1808, is 178ft by 58ft, with an unsupported roof 34ft high.

When in 1811, following his father George III's demonstrable madness, the Prince was elevated to Prince Regent, he decided that he needed a grand palace in Brighton, and he employed John Nash to transform his 'marine pavilion' into a Royal Palace (which it became officially in 1832).

This 'bird's eye view' from the new St Peter's Church around 1828 shows the town stretching towards the coast, 'including the Marine Palace of Her Majesty Victoria the First'. Victoria did not enjoy staying at the Royal Pavilion, and later happily sold it to the borough.

The Music Room, 1826, from John Nash, 'Views of the Royal Pavilion, Brighton'.

Building and alterations lasted until 1822, and resulted in Nash's dismissal in disgrace over the final cost of more than £500,000. The distinguishing features of the one large and four smaller onion-shape domes in Indian style, and the two square wings with concave pagoda roofs, were added during the prolonged period of building. Considering its protracted construction, the completed Pavilion displays a remarkable unity of style.

The Prince Regent, who was crowned George IV in January 1820 on his father's death, formally moved into his palace as king in January, 1821. When the magical and bizarrely exotic interiors were completed George confessed to crying at their splendours, but paradoxically he was to make only a few more visits to his extensive and extraordinary new home.

His brother and successor William IV stayed there, by contrast, at least once in every year of his reign (1830–37). William and his wife, Queen Adelaide, were popular presences in the town – Adelaide Crescent in Hove and Queen's Park in east Brighton are named after her.

Queen Victoria did not, however, find the Indian Royal Pavilion to her taste. Her first visit to the town in October 1837 passed under a giant floral arch spelling WELCOME, and in 1843 she famously arrived at the Chain Pier by boat. But 1845 saw her last visit to the town. Brighton itself she found 'quite a prison'. Royal patronage of Brighton was temporarily at an end, and in 1847–8 van-loads of furniture were removed from the Pavilion for further use by the monarchy. It was a cruel ransacking, of both material and symbolic importance.

Extensions to Buckingham Palace were proving costly, and it was suggested that the Pavilion site might be sold to recoup some money. Proposals that the buildings should be destroyed, or occupied by Brighton College (founded in 1845), came to nothing, and in 1850, after prolonged wranglings, the 9-acre Royal Pavilion estate became the property of the town at a bargain price. Their warm welcome rebuffed and their Pavilion ransacked, the townspeople never again held Victoria in great affection, although the passage of time did lead to their erecting the Clock Tower at the foot of Queen's Road to mark her golden jubilee in 1887.

The Pavilion and its ancillary buildings have enjoyed varied roles under the town's ownership. The Dome and Corn Exchange were used for some years as cavalry barracks, and the Dome was redesigned and opened in 1867 as an assembly hall. The present Church Street entrance was added in 1901, and in 1934–35 the Dome was again remodelled as a concert hall with 2,100 seats. The Dome and Corn Exchanges acquired their names in the 1860s, when the latter became the town's corn market. Since the first world war the Corn Exchange has been used for exhibitions and receptions.

The public was admitted to the Pavilion grounds soon after the town take-over in 1850, and ratepayers were allowed free entry into the Pavilion on two days every month. Variously used for civic functions, as an art school, museum and library, the whole estate was taken over during the first world war as an Indian military hospital, apparently at the suggestion of George V.

The distinctive South Gate, in Gujerati style, was opened in 1921 as a memorial, subscribed to by the 'princes and people' of India. The Indian government also paid for a memorial, the Chattri in Patcham, on the site where the bodies of Indian soldiers who had died from wounds were cremated. It is dedicated to those who had died fighting a foreigners' war in a foreign land. Town folklore has it that when those Indian soliders who survived their wounds came

Richard Henry Nibbs: 'The Landing of Queen Victoria at Brighton Chain Pier in 1843'. Not only did Queen Victoria take a dislike to the Royal Pavilion, but she removed many of the its precious artefacts. During Elizabeth II's reign many have been returned to their rightful home.

to and gazed at their surroundings, they thought that they were in paradise.

After the first world war, the Pavilion was gradually restored. George V consented to return some of the original fittings from Windsor Castle. After 1946 a series of Regency exhibitions was held, and in 1955 Elizabeth II returned over a hundred pieces of original Chinese-style furniture, with further items coming back in subsequent years. Despite misfortunes, including an arson attack in 1975 and a crashing minaret in the great storm of 1987, the Royal Pavilion is now in its finest state for 150 years, while the Dome (*below*) re-opened for concerts in the spring of 2002.

George Canning, the former prime minister, was one of many celebrated figures to settle in the town. An early housing development in this period was Royal Crescent (*opposite*), fourteen seafront houses started in 1798 for 'fashionable visitors' to buy. Their black mathematical tiles have stood the test of time with remarkable fortitude.

Celebrated architects arrived with the high class inhabitants pouring into the town. Charles Barry, Henry Holland, William Porden and James Wyatt all joined Nash in working on the Prince's and other projects, but it was three local architects – Charles Busby, Amon Wilds and his son, Amon Henry Wilds – who were to make a far greater overall impression, their influence being felt especially on the stuccoed buildings extending along the seafront. The creation of Regency Brighton is their achievement. They built not only the grand individual houses and terraces, but also the crescents and squares which serve as the 'bookends' and defining characteristic of the town when viewed from the sea. They were heavily influenced by the cream buildings and pillared facades of John Nash in Regent's Street and around Regent's Park in London. In contrast with Bath or Cheltenham there was no local stone for the builders to quarry, so a compound brick was manufactured and then rendered with plaster (stucco) to look like stone before being painted cream or white. The style was not always popular: not until Osbert Sitwell's book on Brighton in the mid 1930s did it come to be fully appreciated.

The 1820s was the most active decade for Regency building in Brighton. Busby, already associated with stucco moulding and large semi-circular bays, arrived here in 1820. He quickly formed a partnership with the Wilds, father and son, and in 1823 he found himself a ready financial backer in the local MP and businessman Thomas Read Kemp.

St George's Kemp Town was built by Charles Busby for Thomas Read Kemp.

Royal Crescent: a masterpiece of Regency housing development in Brighton.

Their ambitious plans for Kemp Town (*overleaf*) were realised only in part, with 106 houses built of a planned 250. Often sold as carcasses, with only the façade complete, the houses generally had five floors, with public rooms on the first two and bedrooms above. Servants were housed either in the basement or on the top floor, which had smaller rooms. The interiors took 25 years and more to be completed, which explains their wide variety.

The striking St George's Church (*opposite*) was built for Kemp by Busby. Its erection was not without its mercenary motive: Kemp as owner could look to enjoy a regular income from pew rental. His finances had come under mounting pressure, accounting for the scaling down of the original plans. He moved into one of the first completed houses but was broken financially by the strain. The London builder Thomas Cubitt, renowned for his work in Belgravia, now became involved. Having bought land from Kemp on the west side of his estate, Cubitt not only salvaged much of the original grand design, and assured its quality and style, but was also responsible for the completion of the seafront Esplanade in 1835, with Marine Parade giving access not just to Sussex Square but to Rottingdean beyond. The building of Kemp Town inspired the development in 1834 of Brunswick Town to the west, beyond Regency and Bedford Squares.

And what, indeed, of Hove? First mentioned in a record of 1288, it remained a small fishing community, eking out its existence according to the vicissitudes of the fish trade. As late as 1825 it contained only 300 parishioners. When Brunswick Town was developed in the late 1820s, it was considered to be part of Brighton.

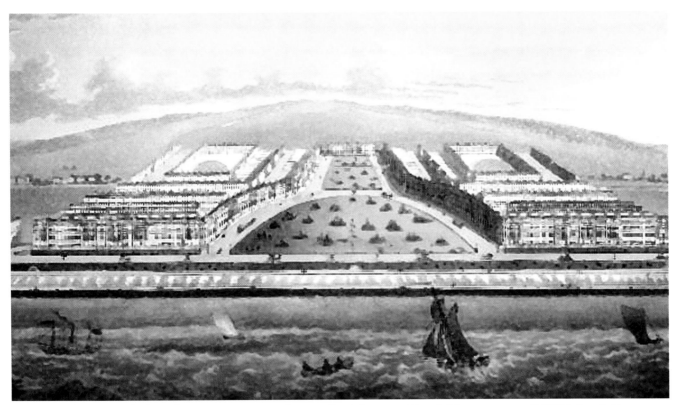

Above: The grand plan for Kemp Town, drawn for Thomas Read Kemp around 1820 by J. Bruce. Note the Downs behind, where the racecourse was soon to be built, and Eastern Road (inland, left) leading off to the west. The plan was not fully realised.

Below: A view of the completed Lewes Crescent, with the Chain Pier on the left and the new Palace Pier behind it. In around 1830 a tunnel was excavated to the esplanade from the private gardens of Lewes Crescent and Sussex Square..

The first building in Hove itself came after 1850 with Cliftonville, and only towards the end of the nineteenth century did Hove become constituted as a distinct geographical and political entity.

Many distinctive buildings in Brighton date from this quite extraordinarily rich period in its history. Wilds junior was responsible for Hanover, Park and Montpelier Crescents, while Thomas Cooper, a builder-architect, designed Brighton Town Hall and the Bedford Hotel. Charles Barry was appointed in 1825 by Thomas Attree to design houses on land he had acquired in 1825 in Queen's Park, in which the Royal German Spa had been opened that year.

Queen's Park: Thomas Allom's painting of 1835 shows how Thomas Attree intended the area to develop.

Kemp's continuing financial woes led him to sell his land in West Brighton to Sir Isaac Lyon Goldsmid (later Lord Palmeira), the first Jewish baronet. He employed the distinguished architect Decimus Burton, who had worked with Nash at Regent's Park and had built the Athenaeum Club in Pall Mall. Beyond the south-east corner of Adelaide Crescent (*p. 48*), however, Burton contributed disappointingly little. It was left to other architects to complete his work, giving the variety of styles – Regency, Italianate, Greek Revival – characteristic of the west Brighton and Hove seafront today. Cubitt's work, meanwhile, was also seen in Belgrave Place (1846) and Clifton Terrace (c. 1850), late flowerings of the Regency style already drawing to a close. The streets were now becoming safer, as gas lights replaced oil lamps: they first came to the Steine in 1824, and by 1853 there were 947 in the town.

If this period in the town's evolution saw its grand properties emulating those of London, paving the way for the later sobriquet 'London by the sea', it also saw the dawning of the town's enduring reputation for loucheness. In the prince's wake came young courtiers and assorted riffraff, whose drunkenness and social mores often scandalised the town. The Napoleonic Wars brought not only soldiers garrisoned here, but also French émigrés, who brought further colour as well as bawdiness.

From this era, too, dates both the Steine in its modern levelled state (a focal point for fashionable society), and the Chain Pier. With the promenade at its head, this soon rivalled the Steine as a meeting point. The end of the Napoleonic Wars in 1815 had revived the need for a more comfortable means of embarking for Dieppe than beach-launched boats could provide. Built by Captain Samuel Brown some 500 yards to the east of the Steine, the Chain Pier consisted of four long spans supported by chains which hung from four substantial supports driven into the seabed. Resembling a massive suspension bridge, it was an impressive sight, jutting a quarter-of-a-mile out to sea, and it inspired the leading artists of the day (*p. 49*).

The Chain Pier was opened to a lavish fireworks display on November 25, 1823. A protective cliff wall against the chalk face of the Downs created the beginning of what became Madeira Drive – completed by the end of the century. The pier was busy at first, with several steam ships leaving daily for France, and for a few years Brighton became the busiest cross–channel embarkation point in England. Queen Victoria arrived at it in 1843 (*p. 42*). In 1847, however, a railway branch line opened to Newhaven, which had protected quays in its harbour in the mouth of the River Ouse. Passengers were lured away, and so died the dream of the town's being the hub of the London–Paris journey.

The Chain Pier was regularly buffeted by strong seas, its solid structure never being wholly sufficient for the task, and it was finally swept into the sea in a severe storm on December 4, 1896. The debris caused considerable damage to the Palace Pier, then under construction, and to the West Pier.

Kemp's financial problems were symptomatic of a troubled 1830s decade for the town, in contrast to the buoyant 'boom' atmosphere of the 1820s. (Kemp himself died in Paris in 1844, a ruined man.) The town's acquisition of two MPs in the Great Reform Act of 1832 provided no magic solution. Brighton suffered, as it did periodically throughout its history, from competition from other resorts, as well as from a national economic recession.

By the time that the Royal Albion and Bedford Hotels opened in the late 1820s the visitors were fading away. The town was no longer fashionable, and building projects foundered as the market became flooded with empty properties. Unemployment and lawlessness rose. By 1830 there were an estimated 18,000 poor in the town – nearly half the population. But as so often happened at a down point, a new opportunity was to arrive, as if from a clear sky, to restore the onward thrust of the town's fortunes.

Adelaide Crescent was designed by Decimus Burton.

Many artists were drawn to Brighton's Chain Pier, among them the two greatest landscape painters of their generation, J.M.W. Turner (above) around 1828 and John Constable (below) a year or two earlier. The pier was still new in this period, but it failed to survive the century.

The Railway Era: 1840s–1860s

Brighton had been a popular tourist resort in the Seaside Resort Era: in 1820, it was estimated that 10,000 visitors, from every class, had come to the town for short or long stays. But the arrival of the train in September 1841, cutting the journey from London from some five to two hours, and in far greater comfort than horse-drawn carriages, opened the doors to mass tourism, including for the first time 'day trips'.

The impact of the trains was swift. In just one month, May 1850, some 75,000 visitors arrived by rail. From the outset commuters to London also moved to Brighton. The following year, *Knight's Excursion Companion* commented that it might almost class Brighton as 'a suburb of the metropolis'. Increasing numbers fled the capital and became daily 'commuters'. Large engineering works by the station called for large numbers of workers and, along with them, cheap dwellings. The railways attracted fresh commerce to the town, helping to bring an end to the late-Regency slump. The censuses of 1841 and 1851 record the population leaping from 46,000 to 65,000, and by 1871 it had risen to over 90,000 – a remarkable doubling in just thirty years. The railway had changed Brighton utterly. The town was never the same again.

A great enterprise. The London, Brighton & South Coast Railway 'navvies' completed the line from London to the coast in less than four years.

Something to celebrate: Brighton station opened on May 11, 1840, at the same time as the branch line to Shoreham. The London line was to open in September of the following year, by which time David Mocatta's much more impressive station building in the Italianate style had been completed.

A railway line had first been proposed in the 1820s, but it was not until 1837 that the London and Brighton Railway Act authorised the newly established London and Brighton Railway Company to build the line. Construction lasted from March 1838 until the opening on September 21, 1841. More than 6,000 men worked on the line, aided by 960 horses. Given the size of the undertaking, the engineering feats involved and the limited state of the technology available, the achievement seems quite extraordinary, especially when judged by the duration of major projects today.

Initially six trains ran each way per day, from London Bridge terminus to Brighton. The quicker, first class trains stopped at East Croydon, Redhill, Reigate Road, Three Bridges and Haywards Heath. Within a few years the first non-stop service was introduced, taking just one hour, 45 minutes. The line was fifty miles long, and consisted of five tunnels (three lit by gas from their own gasworks), 99 bridges and the magnificent Ouse valley viaduct, nearly a mile long and 96 feet high.

The chief features of the railway for the town were the carving out from the chalk of a vast plateau on which Brighton Station was erected (*above, and see map p. 8*); the London Road (*p. 53*) and New England viaducts; and the Patcham Tunnel, 488 yards in length, which opened to great acclaim in June 1841.

Travel direct to Victoria Station became possible when the London terminus opened in October 1860. The branch line to Kemp Town, which included the inspiring Lewes Road Viaduct, was opened in August 1869. The line to Hove followed, but its station was called Hove only from 1895.

The London-to-Brighton Line . . .

was a predominant feature throughout the twentieth century. The train service became quicker (slightly) and more reliable (perhaps), but the route to London remained the same as that built in just over three years from 1838–41.

Luxury and glamour was present until late in the century. The first Pullman cars had been introduced in 1875, and the first all-Pullman train in 1881, including a carriage called Beatrice – the world's first railway carriage lit by electricity. In July 1903 the Pullman clocked the then record time to Victoria of 48 minutes, 41 seconds.

The most celebrated of all the trains on the line was the Southern Belle, dubbed 'the most luxurious train in the world'. It even boasted its own (named) platform at Victoria. Re-christened the Brighton Belle in 1934, it retained its distinctive umber and cream colour until 1968–69, when it was repainted in standard colours by British Rail. In 1970 the actor Laurence Olivier, one of Brighton's most celebrated inhabitants, led a famous campaign against the withdrawal of kippers on the breakfast menu. In 1972, however, the Brighton Belle was withdrawn and the carriages were sold, some subsequently being used on the Orient Express.

The century was in other ways, too, characterised by both improvements and limitations. Electrification of the line came in January 1933, and this shortened journey times. In 1987 the fastest scheduled service to Victoria was begun, taking 51 minutes, and the following year a new record time of 38 minutes, 56 seconds was established. Services to Manchester, Oxford and Scotland, and the Thameslink services to Bedford, opened in the 1970s and 1980s. At the same time the Victorian railway station, after protests from the council and others, was spared by the philistines at British Rail, who wanted to replace it with something 'modern and convenient'.

Charles Rossiter: To Brighton and Back for 3/6d, *1859.*

Above: 'The London Road Viaduct', an oil painting of 1840 by John Wilson Carmichael later exhibited at the Royal Academy.

Below: The locomotive sheds at Brighton Station in October, 1908.

An early 20th century view of a busy station concourse. The board gives prices for Bank Holiday excursions from London.

In 1854, Brighton was incorporated as a borough. Before that date it had been managed by commissioners (since 1773) and clerics. No powerful authority provided a clear overview of the town's needs. Lack of land for development and a paucity of cheap housing had pushed rents up unreasonably, creating slums, widespread homelessness and deprivation. No proper water supply or sewerage system was in place. Factories and abattoirs, dotted across the town, operated uncontrolled. The beaches and streets, especially in the old town, were dirty and (often dangerously) polluted.

A report in the 1850s mentioned 325 known prostitutes in the town, 25 of them under the age of 15. Disease was rife (40 per cent of all deaths were of children under five) and drunkenness was common – in 1849 the relatively short Edward Street, leading to Kemp Town, boasted 26 public houses or beershops. Henry Solomon, the town's first chief of police, was murdered in 1844. It was reminiscent of Dickens' London: no surprise then that the great writer made many trips to the town.

The new borough of Brighton, from 1854 (and Hove when it was set up as a separate borough, from 1898), addressed the rising public needs of a large town. In 1854 control of Brighton passed to an elected body of 36 councillors and 12 aldermen. Water supplies and sewerage systems, improved utilities (electricity was taken over by the corporation in 1894) and better roads and housing all followed. Although serious social problems remained, local government has rarely been more effective in the town's history than it was in the late nineteenth century.

The railway era saw the town burgeon for all classes. Antony Dale says the thirty or more years following the death of George IV in 1837 saw the zenith of its fashionability. The need for housing for all classes was met considerably when the vast area once owned by the Stanford family of Preston Manor, stretching from the seafront in Hove to the Ditchling Road, became available for development from the late 1860s. The land enabled Hove's development to the west of Brunswick Town.

The series of avenues, terraces and villas that characterise Hove were built during the 1870s and 1880s. The last two decades of the nineteenth century saw Hove extended north of Grand Avenue, London builder William Willett being one of the several to develop the area in the footsteps of Kemp and other pioneers. Brighton was also developing northwards in these decades, gradually embracing the villages of Preston and Patcham in generally prosaic mid-to-late Victorian architecture.

The rapid development of the town in the wake of the railway spurred church building, associated in particular with another famous Brighton father and son, Harry Mitchell Wagner (1792–1870) and his son, Arthur Douglas Wagner (1824–1902), both of them vicars. They were advocates of the 'high' church, then engaged in an often bitter 50-year controversy with the sizeable non-conformist 'low' church movement in the town, and they were fired by a missionary zeal. St Peter's, on the Level, designated parish church of Brighton in 1873 to replace old St Nicholas, was H.M. Wagner's first. The finest ecclesiastical building in the town, it is one of our top ten buildings (*p. 66*).

Church building had occurred rarely in the less pious Regency Era. But the number of Anglican churches soared from 14 to 27 from the 1840s to the 1860s, eleven of them commissioned and financed by the Wagners. The dominant style also shifted from the classical (evident in St George's, Kemp Town) to Gothic revival. In contrast to Kemp's church, the Wagners provided rent-free pews for the poor.

The battle of Gothic and Classical designs was seen in the competition held for the building of St Peter's church, the Gothic designs of Charles Barry being chosen in preference to the classical designs from the prolific local Wilds-Busby partnership. The Wagners employed several celebrated architects of national renown, including R.C. Carpenter, who designed St Paul's church in West Street, but also local architects, including Edmund Scott, who designed the controversial and impressively tall St Bartholomew's church (*right*) from 1872–1874. Others to work in the town in this era included George Gilbert Scott, later architect of the Foreign Office and the Albert Memorial, who built Brighton College – an institution founded by H.M. Wagner.

The Jewish community burgeoned, especially with the development of Hove. The work of Goldsmid, and the presence from the 1870s of an important Jewish family, the Sassoons, stimulated migration into a town which had long had a small Jewish presence – the first synagogue, around 1792, was situated in Jew Street, just to the north of the old town. Sir Albert Sassoon and his son Edward were buried in an Indian-style mausoleum in Paston Place, Kemp Town. Stripped of its corpses, the oddly-styled building is now, incongruously, part of a public house.

Hotel building, for both the wealthy and humble, now burgeoned. Most famous of all was Muttons Hotel and Restaurant, opened in the 1840s and remembered in Cuthbert Bede's novel *Matins and Muttons*. By 1860, seaside resorts had become major features of Victorian life, a phenomenon confirmed in 1871 with the introduction of the August Bank Holiday. As that important town historian Clifford Musgrave has written: 'The excursion train brought about the downfall of Brighton as an exclusive resort of the wealthy and fashionable society, and its rebirth as the truly democratic pleasure resort of modern times.'

The railway thus ushered in not only the town's fourth, but also its fifth era, which was one that extended its finger into the twentieth century – the Gaiety Era.

The imposing St Bartholomew's church, off London Road, has a magnificent interior.

The West Pier . . .

has been described as the supreme example of Victorian pier-building in Britain. Designed by Eugenius Birch, the celebrated pier architect, it has not always had a smooth history. Construction began in April 1863 with cast iron screw piles being driven into the sea bed, and it was opened in October 1866. Built with the primary purpose of promenading, it was one of Britain's first pleasure piers, built in the same decade as Bognor, Deal and Aberystwyth.

The initial conception bore only a pale resemblance to the pier that subsequently emerged. The entrance was flanked by two square buildings, much disliked by residents of Regency Square: the only structures out to sea were two octagonal kiosks in the middle of the pier and four octagonal kiosks in either corner of the large pierhead platform at the end.

Competition from the incipient Palace Pier may have provided the spur for the central windshield (added in 1893) and a pavilion seating 1,400 on top of the enlarged pier head. The pavilion was converted into a theatre (1903), and there was a central concert hall (1916) and a raised entrance at the shore (1932).

Between the wars the pier was a popular embarcation point for France and for pleasure trips. During the war the pier bore anti-aircraft guns and was cut in two to deter an enemy assault. Conversion of the theatre into an amusement arcade post-war did not combat dwindling trade. The sea end was closed in 1970, and the whole pier closed in 1975 amid active discussion among the council about demolition. The total cost was to have been £300,000. To have let this happen would have been a tragedy – the worst example of all the terrible losses the town has endured. Tenacious protesters warded off the risk in the 1970s, while the creation of the West Pier Trust in 1978 gave the means to fight on its behalf. Plans that have been billed as 'the last chance to save the West Pier' are being actively considered by the council. As the country's only Grade I listed pier, and the only major one to remain substantially unaltered since the first world war, it must under no circumstances be allowed to be lost to the town and those who visit it.

The pier's historian, Fred Gray, has captured some of its peculiar mystique: 'Part of the enchantment of the pier is that it uses but transcends three environments. It rests on the seabed, but is not part of the sea; it comes from the land, but is landless; it is in the air, but is not airborne.'

The Gaiety Era: 1870s–1910s

Gaiety Brighton, which flowered in the fifty years up to the first world war, can be said to have begun with the opening of the Oxford Theatre music hall in 1863. This was an era for Brighton of gaiety and abandon, of style and imagination, of social deprivation and profound inequality, with the classes rarely meeting, an age of celebration of human endeavour in all its forms – literary, technical,

The Alhambra after its conversion into the Palladium Cinema. It was eventually pulled down to make way for the Brighton Centre. The programme on the facing page is from March, 1904.

artistic, sporting, spiritual and hedonistic. Nationally, it saw moves towards votes for all and of mass trade unions. It was the era of everyman, and every class's needs (and vices) were catered for in the ever-burgeoning town.

Brighton's first theatre had been a barn in Castle Square, used from 1764–70. The first permanent theatre was erected in North Street in 1774. It transferred to Duke Street, where it adopted the name Theatre Royal in 1805 after a visit by the Prince of Wales, before moving to New Road the following year. Much altered over the years, it remains in New Road to this day. Almost every great British actor and actress over the last two hundred years has performed on its stage.

The golden age of the music hall in Brighton is said to have occurred between the 1860s and the end of the century. The Oxford Theatre of Varieties, close to the Theatre Royal in New Road, began offering 'good quality' music and singing, as well as acrobatic and gymnastic performances, from the summer of 1863. Under several names, including the Brighton Empire, it offered variety performances until it closed as a theatre in 1955: it was demolished in 1964.

The Alhambra, with an inauspicious shop-front entrance on the seafront a hundred yards from the Grand Hotel, opened in October 1888. With seating for two thousand in richly cushioned chairs, this elegant music hall theatre was the creation of the tireless theatre architect Frank Matcham. In 1912, it was converted into a cinema, before being pulled down in 1963 to make way for the Brighton Centre. The Grand Theatre on North Road, converted from a circus in 1891–94, also seated an audience of 2000. It survived, offering variety, until 1955, before being burned down in 1961: the site is now a car park. The longest surviving music hall theatre was the Hippodrome in Middle Street, built by Matcham in 1879 and a regular venue for Brighton's variety entertainer Max Miller. Laurel and Hardy performed there in 1952 and 1954, and the Beatles in the 1960s, before it closed as a theatre in 1965.

Brighton's two new piers, like the music halls, aimed to provide popular entertainment as well as exercise for the fashionable. The West Pier was opened in 1866 as a promenade pier, a mile west from the still standing Chain Pier. The Palace Pier followed 25 years later, its creation conditional upon the taking down of the now redundant and decrepit Chain Pier. In 1901 a landing stage was built at the sea-end and the Pavilion Palace was created, decorated with four large minaret towers in imitation of the Royal Pavilion and housing dining rooms and a theatre hall. The new pier later incorporated two toll-booths from the Chain Pier half way along on either side. At 1,650 feet it was Britain's longest, and it rapidly established itself as Brighton's premier tourist attraction, with two million visitors in 1939.

The pier has now become a popular entertainment attraction. The concert hall, built at the north end in 1910, has survived, albeit converted into an amusement centre, but the Pavilion Theatre has not endured.

Brighton Aquarium, which opened in 1872, was conceived by Eugenius Birch, designer of the West Pier. Italianate in design, it extended 700 feet to the east from its entrance on the junction where the high Marine Parade met the low road to the Chain Pier. Its fish tanks were lit from behind to help impart a sense of

the mysterious, but the prize exhibit was the largest fish tank in the world, 100ft-long and holding 110,000 gallons of water. The Aquarium, given a distinctive clock tower two years after it opened, was a substantial building. Its erection necessitated a new sea wall and promenade – the modern Madeira Drive, then called Madeira Road. The Birdcage Bandstand a mile to its west was erected in 1884, an oriental dome supported by an octagon of arches. Few structures better sum up the spirit of the Gaiety Era.

For a brief period Brighton boasted three piers, and this remarkable photograph shows them all: the Chain Pier in the foreground, the Palace Pier under construction and the West Pier beyond..

Volk's Railway, Britain's first public electric railway, opened in 1883 on the seaward side of Madeira Road. Originally running for 300 yards, it was extended the following year to Banjo Groyne, passing under the Chain Pier. In 1896 Volk extended his railway from Banjo Groyne to Rottingdean, devising a curious 'Daddy Longlegs' structure on stilts high above the sea (*p. 100*) that was said to have inspired H G Wells in his *War of the Worlds*. Further groyne construction led to the line's closure four years later, but Volk managed to persuade the corporation to allow him to build a terminus at Black Rock, giving a rail journey of over a mile from the Palace Pier station. The son of a German clockmaker, Volk established the town's first telephone link in 1879, and in 1883–4 provided the Pavilion complex with electricity. He was ahead of his time: not until the 1890s did electric lighting come to King's Road, Madeira Drive, Marine Parade, Western Road and other major streets, and not until the early twentieth century was electric street lighting commonplace in the town.

The sea featured prominently in the Gaiety Era. Sea-bathing remained popular, not just for recreation but as a source of health-giving exercise. Brighton's sea-air was seen as life-enhancing, not just for day trippers and commuters, but increasingly for the retired, now a growing group in society. Promenading became more popular than ever. King's Road and Grand Junction Road were widened, and Madeira Drive was completed in 1872. The terrace almost a mile long above it and along Marine Parade was built in 1890–97. Walking, and being seen, was not just a seaside activity: three of the town's finest public open spaces were created in this era: Preston Park (1883), Queen's Park (1892) and Victoria Gardens (1896).

Sport, too, took off. Brighton had enjoyed one of the leading cricket sides in the county from the mid-eighteenth century. Play was originally on the Steine until ball games were banned in 1787: the game then moved to the Level, where the Prince of Wales' ground was laid out in 1791. In 1823 it moved to the Hanover Ground, then the Brunswick Ground, before a final move was made to the County Ground – on a nine acre site acquired from the prosperous Stanford family – in 1872. Sussex, the oldest county cricket club in the country, have played there ever since.

Brighton United, the town's first professional football team, also played at the County Ground from 1898. The Club rapidly changed its name to Brighton & Hove Albion, and moved to the Goldstone Ground in Hove in 1902–3. Horse-racing had taken place in Brighton since 1783, with the Prince of Wales an enthusiastic patron. In the 1880s–1890s the racecourse, then at a high point in its popularity, was bought and extended by Brighton Corporation.

Brighton's two most celebrated hotels prospered in this era. The Grand Hotel was not only the largest hotel in the town, with 150 rooms, but the tallest, at eight stories. Italianate in style, and crowned by two protruding towers

Volk's Electric Railway c. 1905. Note the bathing machines 'parked' on the right of the picture.

(which have since lost their symmetry due to the building being extended west in the 1980s), it boasted all modern conveniences, including electric lights and lifts – known as 'ascending omnibuses'.

The Metropole to its west followed a generation later. Like the ocean liners then being built, it offered conspicuous luxury. With 328 rooms, it was the largest hotel in Britain outside London. Its distinctive red brick and terracotta made it the first seafront building to break with the traditional cream colour. Some of the most attractive features were on the roof (the bronze spire, turrets and cupolas), but they were removed in 1960 to make way for two extra storeys. The building was designed by Alfred Waterhouse, also responsible for the town hall in Hove. Its style is undoubtedly elegant, but one can legitimately ask whether it was the right building for the prominent position it enjoys: the breach with the white and cream provided a bridge-head used all too eagerly by later developers who rushed in to despoil the unity of the seafront with buildings that lacked the Metropole's aesthetic qualities.

By 1901, the population of Brighton was above 120,000, or 160,000 including Hove. Suburbs apart, much of today's city had been built. As the century ended, the pace of change briefly slowed, the empty state of various seaside buildings being a harbinger of the torpor that characterised too much of the twentieth century. But the new century also ushered in an Indian summer in the town's fortunes. Edward VII, one of our more dissolute monarchs, enjoyed coming to Brighton, and the town repaid his valued patronage by naming the eastern end of the seafront King's Cliff after him.

The Hotel Metropole opened in July 1890.

Harry Preston, one of the town's more charismatic figures, bought the Royal Albion and restored its fortunes. He was also the driving force behind the first motor speed trials on Madeira Drive, which later became the finishing point for the London-to-Brighton Veteran car rally and several other events. In 1910 Preston flew over Brighton in a plane modelled on Bleriot's famous monoplane; the following year Shoreham runway opened as Brighton's official airport; and in 1913 a seaplane station was established at Banjo Groyne.

Tourists increasingly made the journey here by car, while trams also experienced a boom. Special trains brought tourists directly from Manchester, while the Southern (later Brighton) Belle luxury service began in 1908. The crowds in August 1909 were reputedly the largest in the town's history.

Edwardian Brighton remained largely gay and carefree, which is why this chapter ends with the first world war – a conflict that brought the shutters sharply down on two glorious centuries for the town.

Early speedsters pass the FINISH sign as they race along Madeira Drive.

The City's Top Ten Buildings

All the buildings ranked in order below pre-date the twentieth century. This was not by design: no comparable candidates built after 1900 measured up. Indeed, even if the list had been doubled or trebled, no twentieth century buildings would have been included. The list has been drawn up to reflect a cross–section of buildings with a variety of functions: private and public, lay and ecclesiastical, educational and entertainment.

Montpelier Villas and Terrace

The list begins with a fudge, since it was impossible to decide between the merits of Montpelier Villas and the Terrace. Situated in the Clifton Hill area, a triangle between Western and Dyke Roads built in the 1830s and 1840s, they represent the last flowering of Regency in the town. Montpelier Terrace is made up of three-storey houses, with balconies and Ionic pilasters. Montpelier Villas (*below*) is a separate road, lined with semi-detached Italianate villas which have ironwork balconies and verandas. The proportions are delightful: they are some of the finest urban domestic architecture one sees anywhere.

9 Brighton College

One should never discount bias, but it does seem that Brighton College deserves to be placed in the top ten, albeit near the bottom. The main building is by George Gilbert Scott (1849–59), and is an excellent example of Victorian gothic (Scott's preferred style) faced in Sussex flints. Particularly fine are the chapel, the library with its south-facing oriel window, the dining hall and the headmaster's house. The long building in the south and south-west (*right*), making the central courtyard, is by Thomas Jackson (1885-7), who also greatly extended the chapel in 1922 as a memorial to former pupils killed in the first world war.

8 Grand Hotel

Brighton and Hove boasts several fine hotels. The Grand is the only one to be listed here, but the Old Ship and the Royal Albion (very well restored after a fire in 1999) were other contenders. The Bedford would have ousted the Grand had it not been destroyed, and the Metropole is relegated because of its colour and unattractive two storey additions of 1960, which removed the spire. The Grand (1862–4) is striking from the sea, and contains fine interiors, above all a fine staircase (*left*). The external symmetry of the hotel was compromised when it was extended westwards in the renovation that followed the IRA bomb of October 12, 1984.

7

The Hippodrome

Opened in 1897 as an ice rink, the Hippodrome in Middle Street was soon converted into a circus and theatre by that famous theatre-builder Frank Matcham. It hosted not only great actors and actresses, including Sarah Bernhardt, Lillie Langtry, Charlie Chaplin and Laurence Olivier on his debut, but concerts by the Beatles and Rolling Stones in 1965. Much of Matcham's original work remains, including the richly decorated oval dome over the auditorium. It is listed because it is Matcham's only surviving theatre in the city (albeit as a bingo hall), and because it was his finest theatre in Brighton.

6

St Peter's Church

The city has many fine churches: too many to list. St Nicholas's Church is a jewel, and could have been chosen because of its unique historic importance and the beauty of its tower – 40ft tall and dating from fourteenth century. But it is eclipsed by St Peter's, built on the Level in 1824–28 as a chapel of ease to St Nicholas's. This is a building of national importance, being one of the earliest and finest Gothic revival churches in Britain, designed in the decorated and perpendicular styles. The original church was built in Portland stone to Charles Barry's designs, with a fine vaulted ceiling: a planned spire did not materialise. When it was extended northwards and altered heavily in 1848–1902, a Sussex sandstone was selected, giving a marked difference in exterior colour. The design harmonises well, and St Peter's (*below* c. 1912) is a striking and attractive presence in the city.

5 Brighton Station

One of the greatest successes of the conservation movement in town was the saving of the station in 1973–75 at a time when philistines in British Rail were intent on replacing masterpieces of nineteenth century artistry and engineering by late twentieth century functional dross. David Mocatta, architect of the station (1841), and much of the line to

London, too, was a student of Sir John Soane. His terminus building, facing south down what became Queen's Road, was in the Italianate style popular in the 1830s and 1840s. The three storeys were fronted by an elegant colonnade with nine arches. Much of Mocatta's façade has been obscured by the current canopy and entrance, and the colonnade has been removed. His station workings on the platform side had to be sacrificed when the volume of trains (50 a day by 1850) dictated more platform space. In this case, however, change was to the good: the magnificent glass arched roof was built in 1882–3. Nearly 600 feet in length, it has two large and one small iron and glass spans, resting on iron columns. Some £18 million has been spent in recent years on restoring the station and its roof.

4 Brunswick Square

Brunswick Square is one of the finest Regency squares in Britain. Developed in Brunswick Town (before Hove was given its separate designation), it was designed as an equivalent area of upper class housing to Kemp Town in the east. The concept of living in a self-contained house which looked as if it was part of a neo-classical palace had first been employed in Bath, and then in Regent's Park in London. The houses were all of five storeys, with servants living on the top floors and with mews behind for coaches and horses. The sea-facing Brunswick Terrace was the first part to be built, and was almost entirely let as

furnished houses for the season. These boasted symmetrical facades modelled on John Nash's London terraces. Brunswick Square itself was built from 1825–28 and the houses sold for private purchase. The development was intended to be self-contained, having its own church and market (now beautifully absorbed into the Market Arts Centre). Brunswick Square, painted today in yellow cream, remains a place of harmony and beauty.

3 Lewes Crescent

Brighton and Hove has many fine squares and crescents. Lewes Crescent, which forms the bottom part of Sussex Square, is the city's finest. Designed by Wilds and Busby, it is 200 feet wider than the undeservedly much better known Royal Crescent at Bath. One experiences the same sense of harmony and elegance found in Brunswick Square (also by Wilds and Busby) , but the crescent shape which breaks into the square beyond it offers an even more satisfying visual experience.

2 Pavilion, Dome, Museum, Corn Exchange

The Pavilion is one of the country's best known buildings. With the Dome, the Museum (built in the 1830s on the orders of Queen Adelaide) and the Corn Exchange, it forms part

of the finest collection of linked buildings in the city, and one of the most curious, yet appealing, anywhere in Britain. The Pavilion's south gate is Indian not only in style, but in provenance, too. It was designed by Thomas Tyrwhitt in Gujerati style, and carries a simple, but moving, inscription: 'This gateway is the gift of India in commemoration of her sons who, stricken in the Great War, were tended in the Pavilion in 1914 and 1915.' His Highness the Maharajah of Patiala dedicated it for the use of the inhabitants of Brighton in 1921. Our photograph shows the Pavilion's porte clochere.

1 The West Pier

The Pavilion, or indeed any of the other nine buildings or groups of buildings in this section, could have been built anywhere inland. The West Pier, designed by Eugenius Birch and constructed in 1863–66, could only have been built on the sea, into which it stretches well over a thousand feet. It used to be illuminated at night, and one of its early attractions was a miniature cannon fired by the sun's rays at midday. Coupled with its extraordinary beauty and sensitivity, this helps justify its selection here as the best, most beautiful, enduring and important building in the city.

3

THE 20TH CENTURY: IN SEARCH OF A ROLE

The twentieth century saw just three eras, the last of which is nearing completion as city status has been achieved. In contrast to the glorious two centuries which preceded it, the twentieth was often lacklustre. There were some highs, certainly, but for Brighton and Hove the century was too often characterised by a lack of vision and leadership: indicatively, only two of our top ten 'great Brightonians' were twentieth century figures.

The century left behind not one outstanding building, and it destroyed countless of real beauty and value in acts of barbarism and philistinism. It saw other cities in Britain and abroad forge ahead of it – cities with vision, boldness and leadership. It too often allowed mediocre people with poor ideas to hold sway. It let an image of sleaziness and dinginess become popular perceptions of Brighton, insufficiently balanced by the equally valid images of the town as vital, creative and extraordinarily beautiful, unsurpassed outside London. It was slow to counter the loss of the tourist trade to resorts overseas, and it let towns with far less history creep up on it. But opportunities now exist for the city to recover its former glories and rediscover itself.

The opportunity must not be lost.

Suburban Dreams: 1910s to 1940s

The first world war was a boom time for the town. As during the Napoleonic wars a century before, it filled up with soldiers and with visitors such as Vera Brittain, who learned of her fiancé's death while awaiting him in the Grand Hotel on Boxing Day, 1915. The Pavilion and Dome were taken over as a hospital for Indian troops, and the Poor Law Institution (which became Brighton General Hospital in 1935) was re-named the Kitchener Indian Hospital.

But with the Armistice in November 1918, a depression settled over the town. The returning soldiers often could find no work, while many Brighton and Hove families were robbed of their breadwinners and had to scrimp on meagre pensions. Unemployment rose as the fashionable rich went off to the Riviera and beyond, and while towns in the rest of the country benefited from new factories making electrical goods, cars and

machine tools, Brighton failed to persuade large companies to locate here. A large underclass, living in rotting accommodation and with few prospects of permanent jobs, posed a serious problem for the Council.

Into this breach stepped the most remarkable Brightonian of the century, Herbert Carden. A firm believer in 'municipal socialism', from the moment he became a town councillor in 1895 he persuaded the council to become pioneers in civic enterprise, including corporation electricity, telephones, trains and housing estates. Carden was Brighton's answer to Birmingham's Joseph Chamberlain.

From the late nineteenth century Carden had been buying up farmland on the outskirts of Brighton and Hove, including land at Devil's Dyke and Hollingbury that he sold to the corporation at cost. This foresight not only ensured a swathe of 'green belt'

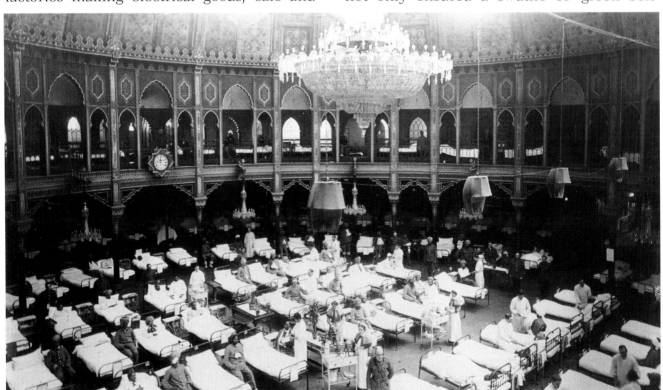

Above: Injured Indian soldiers in the first world war hospital at the Dome.

Page 70: The tower block of the Royal Sussex County Hospital, built in 1969–70.

Page 71: Sir Basil Spence's University of Sussex buildings were typical of the 1960s.

Above: The North Moulsecoomb Estate was designed to house families moved from Brighton slums.

Overleaf: 'Brighton Front', c. 1920, by Charles H.H. Burleigh, with Regency Square on the left. The council later proposed building a car park in the square.

surrounding the town, but secured water supplies and allowed mass housing on rolling downland to be erected in a variety of estates. These new suburbs were facilitated by the bus and motor car providing ready quick access to the centre of town. Slums were cleared, and in 1922 alone some 500 new houses were built. Not all went to plan. North Moulsecoomb was intended as an estate of model homes for residents from the Carlton Hill slums. In practice the rents often proved too high for local inhabitants, and the houses were snapped up by people moving in from London and elsewhere. The Whitehawk and Manor Farm council estates were also developed from the 1930s.

Carden's greatest triumph came in 1928 with the creation of 'Greater Brighton', embracing the surrounding villages of Rottingdean, Ovingdean, Falmer and Patcham. The town's physical size expanded fivefold to 5,000 hectares: it boasted that it was the same size as Chicago. In May of that year, the Duke and Duchess of York (the future George VI and Queen Elizabeth) laid the foundation stones of the two large pylons marking the entrance to the enlarged borough. (With the A23 now a dual carriage-way, one stands forlornly in the central reservation, although a third is planned.) A Labour supporter, Carden was granted a knighthood by Prime Minister Ramsay MacDonald two years later.

The Pylons were erected as a symbolic gateway to Herbert Carden's Greater Brighton.

73

74

C.H.H. Burleigh

Carden, like many visionaries, had his blind spots. In his case they could be severe. His worst came when he put forward, in the borough's Royal Jubilee Souvenir booklet of 1935, a radical vision for the future of the town – discussed more fully in the following chapter. Carden's plan had some far-seeing ideas, including a university for the town (on the hills by Roedean School) and city status. But his proposal to knock down the Regency frontages of Brighton and Hove and replace them with art deco structures ranks as one of the barmiest plans for the town ever to have been put in print.

Herbert Carden died in May 1941, at his home in Marine Parade, aged 73. The *Brighton Herald* in its obituary described him as 'the greatest figure in the history of modern Brighton…All his life, he had loved Brighton, thought of Brighton, worked for Brighton, served Brighton and preached the gospel of Brighton to the exclusion of any other interest.' The newspaper echoed the thoughts of many. Carden was the architect of suburban Brighton. Thank goodness he wasn't the architect of art deco Brighton.

Cinemas were a major development of this era, although the long association of film with the town pre-dated it. Several pioneers of the new industry of moving pictures lived in Brighton and Hove, including Esme Collings, whose catalogues included films deemed suitable 'for gentlemen only'. As early as 1895, regular film shows were being offered to the public in Hove Town Hall.

The first proper cinemas opened in 1910, the Queen's Electric and the Duke of York's, now the town's oldest cinema. Progress Film produced at least 30 films and ranked Charlie Chaplin among its actors. Shoreham Beach became a fashionable home for film stars, including Anna Pavlova, Cicely Courtneidge and Jack Hulbert. Film-going took off as mass entertainment in the 1920s and 1930s, reaching its highpoint in this era before being eclipsed by television from the 1950s. The Regent in Queen's Road, which opened in 1921 at a cost of about £400,000, laid claim to the title of Britain's first 'super cinema'. Further large cinemas were built in the inter-war years, and became focal points in the town's life – the Astoria, Essoldo, Odeon and Savoy. By the outbreak of the second world war there were 18 cinemas in Brighton.

Theatre-going flourished alongside film-going. As many as six theatres were operating simultaneously in the 1930s. The West Pier offered serious drama, competing with the Theatre Royal, while the Palace Pier offered pantomime, touring companies, pierrot shows and musical comedies. These years also saw the last great flowering of 'variety', with visitors enjoying shows at a host of venues, notably the Alhambra, the Hippodrome and the Arcadia.

During this period tourism reached unprecedented heights of popularity, boosted by the electrification of the railway to London in 1932–3. Queues for trains back to London would stretch on sunny weekends down Queen's Road to the Clock Tower. The new electric trains, which survived long into the post-war world, were

Douglas Fox Pitt: Concert on the West Pier, c. 1916-1918.

An artist's impression of the interior of SS Brighton, which was later turned into an ice rink.

not only cleaner but more reliable than trains pulled by steam engines, and gave a further boost to London commuters moving down to Brighton to escape the metropolis. Other attractions of the period were cheap and effective transport from the town's trams (1901–39) and a clean sea to bathe in.

Tourist facilities were enhanced by the construction of the sea wall and undercliff walk to Rottingdean (1930–33); the Aquarium, remodelled in 1929; the giant municipal rock garden opposite Preston Park, laid out in 1935; and Withdean Stadium which opened in 1936, boasting one of the finest tennis facilities outside London. The extravagant 'SS Brighton' swimming pool, opened in 1934, was decorated inside like an ocean liner (hence 'SS' for steam ship), and it housed the largest covered seawater swimming pool in the world, 55 yards long. The crowds did not come, however, and the following year it was converted into an ice rink. Open-air swimming was the vogue: the Rottingdean pool was opened in 1935, Black Rock in 1936 and Saltdean Lido in 1937.

The era saw some terrible developments too. Prime among them was the spread of Peacehaven, a ribbon of ugly housing benefiting the few (the inhabitants and the property developers) but impoverishing the many who no longer were able to enjoy walking or driving through unspoilt Downs and along chalk cliffs but had to face the relentless concrete going east as far as the Seven Sisters. In Brighton, Embassy Court was erected from 1935–6 on King's Road. An elegant Modern Movement building of ten floors, it is utterly out of place on the seafront. Carden, indicatively, thought that it 'showed the way'. He would have liked a whole series of Embassy Courts along the seafront. Worse still is Marine Gate, built from 1937–39, which unlike Embassy Court has little intrinsic architectural interest. Marine Gate (*p. 79*) and the still more unattractive Courcels block of flats in orange are the first sights that greet the traveller arriving in the city from the east.

Continued on page 82

The City's Worst Ten Buildings

Choosing the worst ten buildings was difficult, not because the choice was so limited but because it was so vast. All those selected have been erected since 1900, which says a great deal – and not only about the idea of progress. Architects, builders and developers have a terrible responsibility, because their creations will continue to delight, or to vex, long after their names have been forgotten.

10 Anson House

It's difficult to select just one from the many soulless buildings that line the west side of London Road (a terrible introduction for visitors to the city) but its grotesque delapidation wins Anson House the prize. Who on earth, one wonders, would be tempted to rent it? What architect with any sensitivity could have imagined that the doorway was attractive and fitted the rest of the building? Why has it been left empty for so long?

9 Phoenix Gallery

This building is ugly, dwarfs its neighbours and is an affront to St Peter's church, which faces it. Delightful nineteenth century dwellings were pulled down to make way for it. Bright blue and glass, it is now in use, incredibly, for art.

8 Brighton Square

Two cobble-fronted cottages and a weather-boarded house were destroyed in order to construct this square. The development won the premier Civic Trust award in 1966. The square lacks any intelligent understanding of place or harmony. An architectural disaster in the Lanes, the centre of the historic city.

7 Marine Gate

This is an eight-storey block of flats, built in 1937–39 to the designs of Maurice Bloom on the cliffs at the easterly entrance to the city. Its ranking in the 'worst building' list is on account of its insensitivity to its position. Did the architect imagine that he was enhancing the town by erecting this welcome to it? Did he not notice that it was the entry lodge at the very portals of the city? The only positive comment is that it is less bad than the monstrous orange block of flats visible to its immediate west.

6 St Dunstan's

This is another building which is not devoid of intrinsic merit but which is placed in utterly the wrong position. Also built in 1937–39, this seven-storey building was apparently meant to resemble a bi-plane. For a nearby example of how a substantial building can harmonise with its surroundings, one has only to compare it with Roedean School (1899), a far happier building that complements – and compliments, rather than insults – the Downs.

5   Sussex Heights

This is a very poor building, not on account of its height but because of its pedestrian and unattractive design. If a building had to destroy the exceptional St Margaret's Chapel (C.A. Busby, 1824) and to top the steeple of St Paul's Church, West Street, so making it the dominant feature of the city's skyline, it should have been a whole lot better than this fourth-rate pile.

4   East Brighton council flats

Sussex Heights is for the affluent who could afford to buy somewhere attractive. Inhabitants of Theobald House and the other council houses in the city had little or no choice but to live there. The first tower blocks were built on Albion Hill in 1960. Better if they had not been built. They need not have been. The 'slums' often could have been renovated and made into attractive homes.

3   Hilton West Pier Hotel

This building has already been lambasted in the first chapter. It is well worth a visit. View it from any angle and one cannot discover a single redeeming feature. One really puzzling feature is the irregular patterning on the front balconies. Did the architect think he was enhancing the building's appearance? In every sense, a disgrace.

2 Marina entrance

Could one imagine such an entrance to a marina in France or Italy? In Poland or even in Albania? Some would list the Marina itself as worthy of inclusion in the ten worst, but it has far too many redeeming features to merit such obloquy. The entrance, however, is pure Siberian brutalism. Damp, stained, grey concrete Colditz. Once safely through this urban Hades, one greets the car park ahead as an object of rare delight, beauty and fascination.

1 Kingswest and Conference Centre

There can be no question as to what are the ugliest, worst and most offensive buildings in Brighton and Hove. The Kingswest Centre (*below*) opened as the Top Rank Suite in 1965. Someone observed that it was odd to have a building by the sea with no window, so a central one was added with stunning lack of taste. The Conference Centre next door was opened by Prime Minister James Callaghan in 1977. The architects, Russell Diplock, displayed no intelligent feeling for the sensitive position in which this building was erected. Verdict: a massive failure of imagination and humanity.

Equally grim is St Dunstan's Institute for the Blind in Rottingdean, also built from 1937–39. Here at least is an interesting modernist structure, but designed by someone with no feeling for the Downs. Neither the mass nor the colour displays any sympathetic understanding of place. The building defiles the Downs. Within Brighton and Hove, this era saw the destruction of many historic buildings. Some were pulled down for necessary road widening, but often fine buildings were ripped down thoughtlessly in order to put up characterless, styleless shops, banks and offices so characteristic of the interwar years at their most grey.

The seediness of these years was reflected in Graham Greene's novel *Brighton Rock* (1938). Brighton Racecourse was a centre for organised crime, with protection rackets operated by London-based razor gangs. The unhelpful title 'the queen of slaughtering places' had already been given to the town following the infamous 'Brighton trunk murders' in 1934. Crime was certainly a problem in the town, but was it worse than other resorts with a large transient population? The case is not proved. Greene's novel, and the subsequent film, nevertheless powerfully conveyed the impression that Brighton was a lawless, sinister place.

The second world war did not provide the fillip for the town of the Napoleonic or Great wars. The town suffered war damage for the first time since the French burned it in 1514. Two hundred Brightonians were killed in air raids. The worst day was on September 14, 1940, when 20 bombs fell on Kemp Town. More than 50 people were killed, including four children and two adults in the Odeon Cinema. The most intense attack came on May 25, 1943, when the town was repeatedly dive-bombed by German fighters. Pedestrians were strafed in the streets, buildings were targeted with incendiary bombs and the London Road railway viaduct was hit. Twenty four people died in the raid.

Brighton was transformed during the war. Because of the fear of invasion, anti-aircraft guns, wire entanglements, searchlights, minefields and machine gun posts were placed along the shore. Sections of the piers were blasted away. Air raid shelters were built in school playgrounds, and the town's art and museum treasures were removed to safety. The larger hotels and several schools were requisitioned. Children were evacuated to safer areas. Hove Baths, built in 1938, were taken over by the Navy and re-named HMS King Alfred. More than 20 local boats took part in the Dunkirk evacuation, including the much loved *Brighton Queen.*

Mass street parties greeted VE Day and VJ Day, and bonfires were lit on beaches rapidly cleared of wartime detritus to encourage visitors to return. The postwar boom in tourism lasted until the 1960s, when taking cheap holidays in reliably sunny climes abroad proved feasible for families on even modest incomes.

A fanciful 1930s view of the Royal Albion Hotel.

Right: Bomb damage in Albion Hill, September 1940. St Bartholomew's Church can be seen in the background.

Below: A ravaged wartime seafront, with barbed wire and tank obstructions in place. A section of the West Pier has been removed to prevent its being used by the enemy as a landing stage.

Above: The passenger boat 'Brighton Queen', a popular feature of the pre-war coastline, played a heroic part in the Dunkirk evacuation.

Below: Sir David Muirhead Bone: 'Whitsunday at Brighton', 1945. There was a post-war boom in tourism, until package tours in sunny climates lured vast numbers of British holidaymakers abroad.

The Locust Years: 1950s to 1980s

If ever the town needed another Herbert Carden it was in the 30 years after Elizabeth II's coronation in 1953. For Brighton and Hove it was no glorious 'New Elizabethan Age' but a time characterised by lack of imagination and philistinism, with the men who ran the town (they were all men) rarely capable of raising their eyes, and with developers, like a swarm of locusts, stripping the town of part of its heritage and wealth. Hardly anyone gave the town a vision, as was occurring in the most successful seaside communities both in Britain and abroad, many of which faced similar difficulties.

There were some very good men running the town in these years, loyal and honest, but they were rarely inspired, nor were they big thinkers, and they did not always stand up to cynical and greedy developers who made millions while giving little back to the town

to compensate for bequeathing it their dreadful buildings.

Four bright developments did occur in these years, however, providing markers for the future. The first was a successful rearguard action against architectural barbarism. Part of the blame for its inception must be laid at the feet of Herbert Carden, who uttered the remark 'Even Sussex Square will have to go', and who described the Pavilion as 'a complete anachronism in a modern age'. From here it was no step at all to Hove Council's incredible announcement in 1945 that it planned to demolish Brunswick Square and Terrace, and that the destructions 'would in no way alter the character of the town'.

A meeting was held in December, 1945 which led to the foundation of the Regency Society with Antony Dale its treasurer and

To the barricades: the ugliness and insensitivity of this disgraceful block on the corner of Regency Square explains the the founding of the Regency Society and other conservation bodies. The corner building in Charles Burleigh's painting on pp. 74–75 was pulled down to make way for it. Note the Metropole in both pictures, with the original spire shown in the painting.

Clifford Musgrave its secretary – both future distinguished historians on the town. The society's aim was to stimulate appreciation of the Georgian, Regency and Victorian periods, and to protect the town's historic built environment. The town's redevelopment plan in Hove, which included plans for high-rise flats and a car park, was dropped. The society went on to organise a series of Regency exhibitions in the Royal Pavilion between 1946 and 1980. A special exhibition in 1950 marked the centenary of the town's purchase of the Pavilion, which was instrumental in acquiring for Brighton the status of one of the 1951 'Festival towns'.

The Brighton Society, a more overtly campaigning group, added power to the conservationist cause after its founding in 1973. Together with the Regency Society it turned the tide in favour of preservation and against replacing historic buildings by high-rise and other ugly scars on the built environment. One particularly far-seeing victory was their defeat of plans for a car park on the Regency Square lawns, ensuring that it was built underground instead.

The second development was the foundation of Sussex University, the first autonomous university to be built outside London since the early nineteenth century. The idea had been in the air for more than 50 years: in 1911 a public meeting at the Royal Pavilion had started a fund to establish a university in Brighton. But the first world war intervened and stopped a plan which was, in any case, some way ahead of its day. The money raised was used instead to buy books for the municipal technical college.

In the last months of the second world war the plan was revived. With the purchase of Stanmer Park by the council in 1947, the ideal greenfield site was found midway between the towns of Brighton and Lewes, seaside guest houses helping to provide the vital student lodgings. Proposals were submitted to the government in 1956, and two years later they were approved – making it the first of the new generation of 'red brick'

The Gardner Arts Centre at the University of Sussex, financed by the Gulbenkian Foundation and Dr Lytton Gardner, was completed in November, 1969. Brighton Festival has made great use of it.

universities. In May, 1959 the University College of Sussex was established, and in 1961 a royal charter raised it to full university status. The first 52 students began that autumn, taught temporarily in Preston Road. The importance of the university to the town has been immense: education is now, with financial services, the biggest employer in the city.

Pivotal in the university's development was John Fulton, former teacher and close friend of Harold Wilson (Prime Minister 1964–70 and 1974–76). Fulton chose Basil Spence, the architect of Coventry Cathedral, to design the university buildings. Falmer House opened in October 1962, with others following regularly thereafter: the round Meeting House of 1966 (*p. 97*) was Spence's most impressive structure, although it had originally been rejected by Brighton's planning committee. Spence combined traditional university elements, such as the quadrangle seen at Falmer House, with modern features found in American campus universities, including modern bricks and concrete, a separation of vehicular and pedestrian traffic and a liberal, attractive use of water and trees.

The university flourished under its early vice-chancellors, Fulton (1960–67) and Asa Briggs (1967–76), the latter building its reputation for interdisciplinary courses and exciting scholarship. After the rapid growth in the 1960s and 1970s momentum slowed, as other universities were founded and introduced new competition for bright students and academics. In the mid–1980s it enjoyed a brief renaissance but then slid back again. In 1997 Alasdair Smith was appointed vice-chancellor, and he has begun to restore the university's standing as a centre for internationally renowned scholarship. Its link with Brighton University for the new medical school in 2002 could be the harbinger of future collaborations, enabling it to be a major academic player.

The Brighton Festival was the third important development of this period. The post-war years saw the decline and often the destruction of first, music hall theatres and then of the cinemas. Much-loved local figures such as Max Miller faded from view. Faster train services swelled the number of commuters and day trippers, but it also brought London's theatres, opera and concert houses and cinemas within much easier striking distance of Brighton residents.

Glyndebourne was now in its long ascendancy and attracting international performers beyond the reach of any local venue, while Brighton Philharmonic Orchestra was struggling to make its way. Against this inauspicious background the Brighton Festival was  founded by Denis Hobden and Ronald Bates. Its genesis, according to a later artistic director, Gavin Henderson, was a festival he and fellow sixth-formers put on at Brighton College. Ian Hunter, already involved with major arts festivals elsewhere, became artistic director and catalysed the embryonic beginnings into the first fully-fledged festival in 1967. He encouraged world-class artists to appear, including William Walton, Arthur Rubinstein and Julian Bream. The opening of the Gardner Arts Centre at the university provided a sparkling new venue.

Arts Council funding began to reduce in the 1970s, however, and the festival fell into trouble. It was viewed locally as elitist, and insufficiently in tune with the town. Gavin Henderson, who had organised the Picasso exhibition for the festival in 1982, took over as artistic director in 1984 and was given one year to make it work. He moved the festival's administration from Bracknell into Brighton, secured new funding and successfully introduced more informal and local elements, including the 'open houses'.

Although funding remains a worry, the re-opening of the Dome in 2002 and the acquisition of city status has given the Brighton Festival a new lease of life. It was a vital ingredient which allowed the town to survive the Locust Years.

The final saving grace of this time was Brighton Marina. The subject of serious local controversy, and some fully justified criticism of its appearance, it nevertheless gave Brighton the harbour that had been discussed for centuries and more. A stone harbour for 200 boats had been tentatively begun in 1806 and abandoned. The Chain Pier, built in 1823 with the quay at its pier-head, met some of the need for deep-hulled boats which could not be boarded from the beach – as did the two subsequent surviving piers – but discussions over a protected harbour continued, especially as trade was steadily being lost to the developing ports of Newhaven and Shoreham. It was not until 1963, however, that Henry Cohen, a local garage owner and yachtsman, proposed his £9 million marina, including mooring for 3,000 boats, a conference hall, a large Caribbean garden, swimming pool, helicopter base and hovercraft port. Local opposition resulted in many delays and the moving of the marina east from Cohen's proposed site to Black Rock.

Work began in 1971, with 110 concrete caissons (giant cones) being dropped into place by a 1,200-ton crane, then the largest in Europe. Each weighed 600 tons and was 38ft high and 40ft in diameter. Local objections resulted in the ruling that the marina buildings should not exceed half the cliff height. The final caisson was dropped into place in May 1976, enclosing 77 acres of sheltered water and containing a large, non-tidal inner harbour by the cliff face. It was opened to much acclaim by Elizabeth II in 1979. Amid high hopes, a jetfoil service to Dieppe started at the same time but was withdrawn the following year. Fresh life came with new owners after 1985, when much of the original inner harbour was filled in. Shops and a 'marina village' with 875

The ugly Thistle Hotel was built on the seafront in the heart of the old town.

homes opened in the first phase of the new development, followed by the cinema and further leisure activities, and from 2002 a hotel and more waterside shops and restaurants. The Marina still has its critics, but without it the town would be much the poorer. It has even provided protected harbouring for the town's remaining fishing fleet, an echo of the first era in the town's history.

For the economic vitality of the town the key development of this era was the Brighton Conference Centre, opened in 1977. With a capacity of 5,000, it helped to keep the hotel trade in business and the town's profile high nationally – above all with the annual party conferences which by the 1970s were demanding far better facilities than had been traditionally offered in the Dome. Blackpool had developed new facilities, and Brighton was facing fresh challenges from towns such as Bournemouth and Harrogate. The centre was needed, but it is the wrong building with the wrong design, the wrong specification and the wrong external colour and texture. Its erection destroyed buildings of priceless value to our heritage. The destruction was justified in this case, because the conference centre needed to be on the seafront and adjacent to the Grand and Metropole hotels. It could have been dug further down into the chalk, however, and the façade designed to blend with, rather than insult, the Regency and Victorian frontages. The design does not allow the flexibility and large exhibition space that today's conferences demand. In every sense it is a very limited and very grey building.

The overwhelming sense of these post-war locust years, the four acknowledged highlights notwithstanding, is one of mediocrity, of dullness, of barren political infighting, of deals with developers and lost opportunities. No significant industry was encouraged into the town to compensate for the winding down of engineering firms: the arrival of financial service companies, most notably American Express, compensated only in part for the job losses. Considering its prime location, the failure to attract more business into Brighton and Hove must be regarded as a major indictment.

The abiding images of these years are of elegant and humane buildings blown away to be replaced by concrete wildnernesses; of 'mods and rockers' fighting with fists and deckchairs on the seafront (*overleaf*); of the ugly £25 million Thistle Hotel (*facing page*), which destroyed part of the remaining streets and houses in the old town; of the (incredibly) award–winning Sainsbury's supermarket on Lewes Road, whose exterior walls sport a feature in cruel homage to the impressive viaduct which was knocked down to make way for a building which ruined the livelihoods of many local shopkeepers; and, finally, of the beautiful West Pier, rotting forlornly against a setting sun.

Brighton Marina: many mistakes were made, but it is undeniably a major asset for the city.

A symbol of the era: mods and rockers fighting by the Aquarium on Whitsun bank holiday Monday, May 18, 1964.

Top Ten Great Brightonians

This is not a list of famous inhabitants of Brighton. Those listed below, whether inhabitants of the town or not, all helped create the town at its best as we know it today. Without these individuals the town would have been immeasurably the poorer.

It is tempting to list the 'Worst Ten Brightonians', those whose greed, lack of imagination and size of ego impoverished the built town and its social fabric. Many candidates present themselves, but good manners, taste and a wish to avoid bad feeling (and lawyers) dictates that the list should be left to the reader's imagination.

1   **The Prince Regent** (*right*), whose patronage helped rejuvenate the town from the 1780s.

2   **Thomas Read Kemp**, the patron of the Wilds and Busby partnership whose grand vision inspired the Regency seafront.

3   **David Moccata**, creator of the sweeping Brighton station and magnificent railway viaduct and bridges.

4   **Dr Richard Russell**, reviver of the town's spirits in the mid–18th century.

5   **Eugenius Birch**, designer of the West Pier and Aquarium.

6   **Magnus Volk**, inventor, railway builder, bringer of light and sound.

7   **The Wagners**, father and son, 19th century church builders extraordinaire.

8   **Frank Matcham**, theatre and music hall architect (Alhambra, Eden and Hippodrome theatres).

9   **Sir Herbert Carden**, architect of inland 20th century Brighton, although also would-be destroyer of Brighton's 19th century seafront

10   **Glynn Jones**, genial impresario of the City Era.

Other worthy candidates are **Sir Isaac Lyon Goldsmid** (later Lord Palmeira), the entrepreneur behind much of Hove seafront, **Thomas Cubitt**, who rescued Kemp Town, the **Wilds/Busby** architectural partnership and **Thomas Pelham** of Stanmer Park.

The City Era: 1980s onwards

Brighton in the 1980s was in the doldrums. Investment was low, unemployment high. A recovery in the late 1980s and early 1990s was initially blunted by severe recession which hit the local economy severely, but it took off again from the mid- to late-1990s. The era is associated in particular with two individuals: Glynn Jones, chief executive from 1989–2001 (one of this book's 'ten great Brightonians'), and Steve Bassam, a student of Sussex University from 1972–76 who later became Labour leader of the council (1987–99).

Bassam has something of Herbert Carden in him. He had a real vision for the city, of a quality possessed by no other post-war leader, and he had the powerbase to put part of it into effect. He wrested control of the Labour group from the Militant Tendency and other purely negative forces, and he imparted a real sense of direction and optimism. Lord Bassam is an over-criticised and undervalued figure in Brighton's history.

Many important developments occurred during this era. Establishing a unified authority for Brighton and Hove in 1997 brought a strategic ability to view the development of both towns as one – which, in truth, they always were. Having just lost out to Sunderland in 1991, Brighton achieved city status in 2000. The revived seafront between both piers provided an important new tourist attraction, transforming a decaying asset into a vibrant one. Bus services were dramatically improved, although transport problems as a whole were not solved.

Churchill Square was re-developed in the late 1990s at a cost of £90 million, replacing the ugly concrete, steel and glass shopping centre of the late 1960s. The £10 million refurbishment of the Royal Pavilion was completed in 1990. Money was obtained for rebuilding the West Pier, the Dome and Brighton Museum and Art Gallery and for building a new library. Hove Museum and Art Gallery was extensively redeveloped.

The new Churchill Square, redeveloped at the close of the twentieth century.

The Museum and Corn Exchange with exterior restoration work almost completed in mid–2002.

Brighton Station was successfully renovated, and a new waterfront development was built at the marina. A new vitality infused Brighton Polytechnic under its energetic director David Watson after it gained new status as Brighton University. Over-ambitious plans for an 'academic corridor' from Brighton to Lewes, and for a Sussex 'silicon valley', were offset by the founding of the Sussex Innovation Centre in 1993 and the joint Brighton–Sussex University Medical School in 2002.

The period's greatest achievement, however, is intangible: a sense of optimism and momentum. A vision arose of a city of culture. Indeed, in 2002 a bid was launched to become the European City of Culture in 2008. In the same year, fittingly, Brighton & Hove Albion, in the doldrums during the 1990s, were promoted to the first division of the football league – and no greater source of local communal pride exists than the Albion.

But this era only laid the foundations for what needs to happen in the future. Without

foundations, certainly, no edifice can stand, but foundations not built upon will quickly be covered by unsightly vegetation. The conservation movement, so vital in the Locust Years, has shown signs of becoming a reactionary force, hampering the city's progress. Without development the city will ossify, and with it the monuments that are rightly loved by the conservationists.

The next few years will be critical. Brighton must make strides towards entering its ninth era, the International City.

A new optimism, a new momentum. Above: Brighton & Hove Albion fans celebrate a second successive promotion, achieving first division football for the city in the 2002–3 season. Below: A rejuvenated lower promenade between the two piers brings to an end years of neglect and decay, creating a new tourist attraction.

The City's Ten Best 20th Century Buildings

Many interesting buildings have been erected in Brighton and Hove since 1900, but none of them achieves greatness and none is a work of art. If modern buildings are to work well in an historic town they must either harmonise in scale, proportion and materials with their surroundings or, alternatively, make bold statements. Few of our new buildings harmonise, and none makes an effective bold statement as does the Royal Pavilion.

The buildings selected here are listed by date of construction. As none of them is of enduring aesthetic quality, it was impossible to put them in an order of merit.

Duke of York's Cinema

Opened at Preston Circus in September 1910, this was one of the country's first purpose-built cinemas, with seating for 800. It was developed for Mrs Violet Melnotte-Wyatt, the lessor and later manager of the Duke of York's Theatre in London, and the architects were the local partnership of Clayton and Black. It has barely altered, and retains its Edwardian baroque facade – although that pair of stripe-clad legs plunging into the roof is a fairly recent, and decidedly wacky, addition. This is an enriching building which stands out as an island of beauty in an otherwise barren part of Brighton.

King and Queen, Marlborough Place

Rebuilt in 1931–32 as an elaborate Tudor extravaganza, it rises above the tattiness of contemporary pub 'Tudorism' because of the successful use it shows of authentic detailing – seen in the carved oak timbers, tapestries and heraldic glass as well as in the external details. Clayton and Black were the architects, while Heaton, Tabb & Co, the well-known firm of pub decorators, were responsible for fitting out the interiors.

Embassy Court

Opened in 1936, this example of the modern movement is vibrant and visually exciting. It is an important building, one of the few of its style in Sussex, and includes the first purpose-built penthouses in England. But it is in utterly the wrong place. If it had to be situated where it was, it should have been built three storeys lower so that it blended in with, rather than upset, its neighbours. Then it might have been a great building. Its horizontal line, too, clashes with the prevailing vertical emphasis of the Regency seafront. The least worthy of these ten buildings, it is the most controversial inclusion.

Saltdean Lido

The lido opened in 1938 and, as with Embassy Court, was influenced by the work of Erich Mendelsohn – especially his designs for the De La Warr Pavilion in Bexhill. There are also clear echoes of Lubetkin (as in his penguin pool in London Zoo). The design is remarkably unified, with distinctive curved walls and glazing, and a horizontal emphasis in handrail and windows. This is a fine monument, and one that contrives to blend admirably into its environment.

Spence buildings, University of Sussex

Basil Spence was commissioned in 1959 to prepare a master plan for the entire new campus. He attempted, with some aplomb, to harmonise key buildings into the gently sloping valley. In some ways his plans disappoint, given his enviable opportunity to build from scratch and with considerable financial resources behind him. Most worthy are the human scale of his buildings, the prevalence of trees, the use of open space and his building of ponds. Too many of the buildings, however, are visually unexciting. *Right*: the Meeting House.

Faculty of Art and Design, Brighton University

Opened on Grand Parade in 1967, and requiring the demolition of several Victorian buildings, this is nevertheless a success. The scale and style works in its setting, and the use of glass and concrete is harmonious, not vulgar. This building demonstrates that the modern can still sit happily beside the Georgian and Regency. Note the contrast with the unattractive Phoenix Gallery (*p. 78*) a quarter of a mile to the north.

Amex House

A controversial choice, but its design works admirably – a white frontage with blue-tinted glass, almost in conscious imitation of the horizontality of Embassy Court. The building, designed by the Gollins, Melvin, Ward Partnership, was opened in 1977 in order to house major European offices for American Express.

Kings House, north extension

Originally built as seven large terraced mansion blocks in 1872, Kings House stands in the south-east corner of Grand Avenue, Hove. It was designed by James Knowles, who was also responsible for the Grosvenor Hotel in London and much of the building to the west of Palmeira Square. It was sympathetically extended to the north in 1981 (*left of photograph*) to the designs of Miller Bourne.

The Aldrich Library, Brighton University

A remarkably successful glass building, completed in September 1996 on the Lewes Road, which stands out like a beacon against the dull or even gruesome neighbouring Brighton University buildings. The architects, Long and Kentish, have designed a light and energy-efficient building, attractive to look at and to work in. It can accommodate up to 450 students simultaneously, using computing, printed or audio-visual resources.

Van Alen flats, Marine Parade

This building, on the seafront just to the east of the Palace Pier, was named after the architect William Van Alen, whose most notable work was the Chrysler building in New York. This is Art Deco in style, and was concurrent with the international movement in the 1920s and 1930s, in which Marine Parade had its roots.

The design was developed with regard for the original building's height, colour and design. The site is angled in plan, with the Europe Hotel stepping forward considerably from the Madeira Hotel, so creating the stepped plan form, each element with a curved bay that echoes the Regency style. The façade is rendered, with the roof being set back, and has a combination of full height glass and grey metal panels – a modern interpretation of the traditional mansard roof.

It has been designed with large glazed areas, balconies and terraces to enjoy the views across the seafront, while retaining the vertical emphasis and form of the surrounding buildings with the use of the fins, which both articulate and give privacy to the individual flats. The introduction of *brille soleil* to reduce solar gain, together with stainless steel and glass balconies, give a lightness to the building. It was opened in 2001.

A SEA VOYAGE ON WHEELS

AT
BRIGHTON.

The
BRIGHTON
& ROTTINGDEAN

SEASHORE
ELECTRIC RAILWAY

FREQUENT SERVICES DAILY.

Cars Start From the
KEMPTOWN STATION
OF VOLK'S
Electric
Railway.

SALOON.

HIGH TIDE.

HIGH

4
IMAGINING BRIGHTON

Few British towns outside London have loomed as large in popular or in artistic consciousness as Brighton. A place of abandon, freedom and excess; a town to simmer in sex if not to sizzle under the sun; a town of danger and drugs but also of history and culture; a town to take one's family and also one's mistress, although not on the same weekend. A place of contrast: a contrary town. Keith Waterhouse famously described Brighton as a town which was 'helping police with their enquiries'.

Brighton and Hove has been painted by artists, including John Constable and J.M.W. Turner, described by poets such as T.S. Eliot and Alan Brownjohn, used as a setting by Jane Austen, Charles Dickens, William Thackeray and countless other novelists, and featured as the backdrop of films as varied as *Brighton Rock* and *Oh What a Lovely War!*

It is clear that there is not one but several cities of Brighton and Hove, overlapping, ducking and weaving in and out of each other, defying definition, rarely meeting.

The Nine Lives of Brighton & Hove

This chapter suggests that there are nine different cities.
The presentation is deliberately impressionistic.

1 DANGEROUS CITY

Brighton's rapid expansion from the early nineteenth century created extensive slums, with drunkenness and prostitution endemic. This image – reinforced by the infamous Brighton trunk murders in 1934 and the reputation for criminality and violence surrounding the racecourse – found its apotheosis in Graham Greene's novel *Brighton Rock* (1938). In the book a young gang leader (Pinkie) carries out revenge killings and then tries to cover up the crime. In the 1947 film version (*below*), Pinkie is hauntingly played by a young Richard Attenborough. The mods and rockers clashes of the of the 1960s (*pages 90–91*), popular images such as the 1990s BBC *Eastenders* 'Brighton special' and the 'drug capital' reputation of recent years have all maintained the impression of a dangerous city.

To those of us who live here, especially refugees from London and other large cities, it is, however, a haven of tranquillity.

A still from the film of Brighton Rock, with Pinkie and Rose walking towards the pier. The town lent itself to Greene's characteristic portrayal of seediness and decay.

2 VACATION CITY

Brighton has been a holiday town for nearly 300 years. While the rich and fashionable patronised it in the mid–eighteenth century, it was the railway in the nineteenth that opened it up to the mass market. Cheap overseas travel in the twentieth century saw the town adapt to short stay holidays. By the early twenty first century, it was marketing itself as 'a city where the season runs from January to December'.

3 HOMESTEAD CITY

The first great pulse of house building beyond the rectangular old town after the 1770s was driven by fashionable society wanting to buy or rent smart stuccoed properties by the sea. Then, from the 1840s, Londoners flooded to Brighton and Hove to commute by train to the capital. A third wave of settlers came in the interwar years, when new homes were erected to attract the middle and professional classes: mass housing estates were built for evacuees from slum clearances in the town, but these were often snapped up by Londoners moving south. A city of proud homeowners, living in their own discrete enclaves, is thus another core ingredient of the city.

4 POLITICAL CITY

Britain's main political parties have been coming to Brighton for their annual conferences since 1924, although it has only been since the 1950s that they became a fixture. Held first at the Dome, and then at SS Brighton (the conference hall was erected over the ice rink, and members complained of cold feet), they have been staged at the Brighton Centre since the 1970s.

Some moments stand out: the Labour party conference in October 1962 with Hugh Gaitskell pledging to avoid the ending of 'a thousand years of history' by keeping Britain out of Europe; the IRA bomb in 1984 at the Grand Hotel, which narrowly failed to kill Mrs Thatcher; a brave but misguided mayor, Jill Sweeting, who denigrated the Tories' housing record in 1992 and gave them a pretext to abandon Brighton as a regular conference venue; and Tony Blair's speech to the Trades Union Congress on September 11, 2001, rewritten to take account of the terrorist attacks on New York and Washington.

Fact and fiction blend in Ian McEwan's script for the film *The Ploughman's Lunch*, which includes sequences shot at the 1982 Conservative party conference.

The devastated Grand Hotel after the IRA bomb during the 1984 Tory party conference.

Brighton Lanes, the heart of the historic town and long linked to louche activities.

5 LOUCHE CITY

As early as 1841 *New Monthly Magazine* claimed that 'Brighton is the most convenient spot in all the south-eastern part of the Kingdom when in search of "a lark", and a great recommendation that is'. Thackerary set *Vanity Fair* partly in Brighton, describing the town as always looking 'brisk, gay and gaudy, like a harlequin's jacket'. Lydia Bennett in Jane Austen's *Pride and Prejudice* says Brighton is 'the place to get husbands'.

The louche image remains – from T.S Eliot's *The Wasteland*, the most influential English poem of the twentieth century, which alludes to a weekend of sex at the Metropole Hotel, through two Carry On films (1971 and 1973) to Keith Waterhouse's recent witticism that Brighton is the place to go for the lover who buys his partner knickers on Victoria Station and has them off two hours later in a seafront hotel.

6 GAY CITY

Brighton, rather than Hove, became closely identified with the gay scene in the 1960s and 1970s, but its origin as a town friendly to gays goes back to the music hall and theatre presence during the nineteenth century, and to the bohemian atmosphere of the town at the *fin de siecle*, associated with artists such as Aubrey Beardsley. The raffish air of the interwar years and the growing student and avant-garde presence after the war further helped contribute to Brighton being seen as a town at home with the unconventional and alternative. The city boasts gay bars, cafes, hotels and shops galore. *The Fruit Machine* (1987) is one of several films shot in whole or part in Brighton portraying gay life. The city's Gay Pride march *(above)* has become a major event on the gay calendar. Brighton is Britain's gay equivalent to San Francisco, without its skyscrapers – yet!

7 HIGH CULTURE CITY

This is the Brighton and Hove of smart theatres and famous actors living in 'London by the Sea'; the setting for novels by Charles Dickens (*Dombey and Son*), Arnold Bennett (the Clayhanger trilogy) and Evelyn Waugh (*A Handful of Dust*); the city which was the cradle of British cinema and is now home to the Brighton Festival; the city which has been painted by many of Britain's finest artists and which boasts some of the country's very best Georgian and Regency architecture.

This is the serious city, which rejoices in its renovated Dome and art gallery, and the museums in Brighton and Hove. This is the image being promoted in the bid to be declared the European City of Culture in 2008.

8 POPULAR CULTURE CITY

Frivolous to some, deadly serious to others, this city exists side by side with the city of high culture. This is the city that supports Brighton and Hove Albion; the city of popular entertainment, represented by the metamorphosis of the Palace Pier Theatre to fun fair; the city of clubs, live music and parties in the park, of bowling alleys, Brighton racecourse and amateur sport. There is an energy here to keep the city young, and to keep renewing it.

Sport is a vital ingredient of popular entertainment in Brighton and Hove.

Above: The County Cricket Ground in Hove.

Left: Brighton racecourse, revamped in recent years, is popular with punters.

9 CITY OF THE EXCLUDED

The city, as has been shown, has always housed a large underclass. Six decades of heavily targeted expenditure under the welfare state has done little to narrow the divides within society. The city has significant problems in meeting the needs of the homeless, and special difficulties over the unusually high numbers of the elderly, many of whom retired to Brighton and Hove. It also has near-chronic problems of long-term unemployment and deprivation, especially in the east end of the city. A deep gulf divides east Brighton from prosperous Hove – a tale of two cities, indeed.

Right: Many slum buildings (like these in the Carlton Hill area) were pulled down during the 1930s, but Brighton still has its sorry pockets of deprivation.

Three Visions of the City

*Brighton is a place that stirs the imagination.
Many people have considered how it could be
improved, and three such plans are examined below.*

CARDEN'S VISION

Best known of all, and the one adorning the inside front cover of this book, is Herbert Carden's celebrated plan, described in Chapter 3 and produced for the town's official souvenir for George V's silver jubilee in May 1935.

Carden imagined a 'City Beautiful' stretching from the mouth of the Adur in Shoreham to the Ouse in Newhaven, to be created within twenty five years – that is, by 1960. He wanted to make Brighton 'one of the most favoured residential resorts in the world', believing that the town possessed 'one of the finest sites in the world'. He envisaged a city with 'noble buildings, fine hotels, modern flats, imposing houses, great university halls'. He was not a man for half measures, or for delay: 'Shall we plan along these lines, and hand over to posterity the City Beautiful, or shall we still think of day trippers and whelk stalls as the destiny of Brighton?'

Carden's vision, if enacted, would have destroyed Brighton and Hove. Most of the historic buildings on the seafront and inland would have been swept away ('many of them, to tell the truth, are extremely ugly and have no pretensions to architecture at all', he wrote). Street widening would have taken place everywhere inland, with the 1930s buildings in Western Road becoming the norm, and the 'mean streets that lie behind the present front' (including the Lanes) razed to the ground. The entire two-and-a-half-mile Regency and Victorian sea frontage would also have been knocked flat, and 'art deco' ten-storey buildings put up in their place: 'Embassy Court has shown us how to build for the new age'. Lewes Crescent, Sussex Square, Royal Crescent, Brunswick Square, Adelaide Crescent and Montpelier Terrace were all to be bulldozed. Oh, and Brighton town hall and the Pavilion were to suffer similar fates, too.

Was he mad? Perhaps a little. This was, after all, the decade in which Albert Speer was coming up with messianic architectural plans for Hitler's thousand year Reich.

Embassy Court dwarfs and insults its neighbours, but Herbert Carden loved it, regarding it as the ideal seafront building.

But Carden's vision should not be rejected out of court. He had some far-seeing and important ideas, including the unification of Brighton and Hove into a single city, a 'University of Brighton' (which he placed on the hills surrounding Roedean School), a more attractive seafront than then existed and a by-pass around the city. He was also right to realise the necessity for dynamic civic leadership, strategic vision and urgency.

Instead, one had the torpor of the post-war years, and a brutalism which swept away much of the historical and the beautiful. Carden must shoulder some of the blame for preparing the ground for such acts of vandalism. He was wrong to believe that the historic had to be swept away in the name of progress. Great cities of the world (which is what he wanted Brighton to be) blend the old with the new.

COHEN'S VISION

The second vision was that of Carden's fellow Labour councillor, Lewis (later Lord) Cohen. Cohen advocated extending Valley Gardens from St Peter's Church inland to Preston Park, so that 'to the sea, a chain of gardens would run right through the valley of the town'. This imaginative plan fell on the hurdle of the extensive number of houses that would have had to be demolished in order to make it possible.

In 1951 Cohen outlined a more wide-ranging vision to Brighton Rotarians, including:

• A conference hall, a concert hall, flats and shops on land between West Street and Russell Square, cleared between the wars.
• A new open-air bathing pool in the centre of town.
• A number of modern hotels.
• A bathing 'plage' on the Hove side of the West Pier.
• A children's playground and music pavilion on the seafront.
• Sun terraces on Madeira Drive in place of the existing coach parks.
• A small harbour for yachtsmen, and better facilities for youth hostellers.

Cohen's ideas were hardly radical, lacking the grand sweep of Carden's, but the early 1950s saw a ferment of ideas. D.J. Howe, the town's borough surveyor, advocated dual carriageways along the seafront from the Aquarium to Hove, separated by a six foot wide island; a restaurant and shops between the bandstand and the Palace Pier; and several underground car parks. The last (an excellent idea) was enacted in Regency Square but not, sadly, elsewhere: new multi-storey carparks were to blight the town instead.

Lack of finance in conjunction with political differences conspired to defeat the ambitious plans of the time. The only development along the seafront in the entire 1950s was a £13,000 bathing pavilion, just to the west of

This former 1950s bathing pavilion is now a popular Italian restaurant.

108

How things might have been: a plan for the redevelopment of the Hotel Metropole in 1965.

the West Pier. Formally opened in 1952 as one of Brighton's contributions to the Festival of Britain, it proved unpopular with bathers. In 1957 it was leased to the Milk Marketing Board, becoming a 'milk bar' for a while before being boarded up. It is now (*facing page*) the popular 'Al Fresco' Italian restaurant.

THE 2008 VISION

The third vision is contemporary, drawn up in 2002 as part of the bid for Brighton and Hove to become European Capital of Culture. The bid, entitled 'Where Else?', is full of energy and imagination, and comes on the crest of a wave of ten to 15 years of progress and activity in the city.

The ideas, to be achieved by 2008, include:

• A new International Convention Centre to replace (or to complement) the 1970s Conference Centre.
• A restored West Pier, with supporting land developments (now in train).
• A major new sports and leisure facility at the King Alfred.
• A new public leisure and recreational development at Black Rock.
• A new Central Library (in train), together with outdoor public performance space.
• A new contemporary art gallery at the University of Brighton.
• A national-class football stadium for Brighton and Hove Albion (in train).

• National Park status for the South Downs (in train).
• A light-rapid-transit system (monorail) – details unspecified.
• Extensive park-and-ride facilities.

The proposals are illustrated in cartoon style by J Ramm, entitled 'Brighton and Hove Where Else? A vision of the city in 2008' (*overleaf*). They are full of intelligence, are carefully planned and have drawn on a wide range of experience across the city. Because they have had to be properly budgeted, the vision is more cautious than would have been the case if the planners had worked without constraints.

The vision of 'culture' is not as broad as it might have been, and could in particular have embraced sport more fully: selling playing fields for development has meant that sports facilities of all kinds need to be built urgently. The 'Where Else?' remit precluded the vision from discussing redress for the city's chronic housing shortage, or the need for new business to boost income generation. The city is hard up, and has been for years: it would not be if international companies which could be taxed heavily were to be brought here. Overall, however, the 'Where Else?' vision is the most far-seeing, practical and constructive set of proposals to have been produced in the town's long history.

My own vision is the subject of the book's final chapter.

Left: Russell Square car park. If the 1960s planners had had their way the city would be scarred by many more eyesores such as this.

Overleaf: The vision for the city in 2008 by the 'Where Else?' campaign.

5

SEASIDE RESORTS IN BRITAIN

Seaside resorts began to grow in Britain from the early eighteenth century, as seabathing became fashionable. Some resorts, such as Brighton and Scarborough, combined bathing with spas. The nineteenth century was a period of growth and prosperity for resorts, boosted by the coming of the railway from the 1830s and the dawn of the mass holiday. By 1900, a series of thriving resorts ringed Britain's coastline.

The twentieth century at first saw continued growth: although the very affluent increasingly travelled abroad, the middle and working classes flooded to the resorts as never before, a process facilitated by postwar holidays-with-pay legislation and higher disposable incomes. Many resorts became seen as desirable locations for retirement.

Although the peak of visitors to most British seaside resorts came in the 1960s and 1970s, competition from cheap package holidays abroad became keen. Their infrastructure built around tourism, the resorts had had little incentive to attract industry. This lack was now sorely felt, and many were hampered by low levels of visionary leadership, political will and investment. Others rose to the challenge.

This chapter briefly examines five of those resorts. Two of them are slipping, two are benefiting from strong strategic leadership and one is doing spectacularly well.

BOURNEMOUTH

Brighton's chief rival is Bournemouth. The latter enjoys one great advantage over its neighbour along the coast – its seven miles of sandy beach. But this is outweighed by Brighton's advantages, principally its proximity to London, the beauty of its buildings and its history.

Bournemouth was established only in 1810, and until the 1870s it was insignificant, with a population of only 2,000. By 1881, with the advent of the railway, this had soared to 16,000 and by the outbreak of the first world war it had climbed to 80,000. Bournemouth did well between the wars, but after 1945 it suffered, along with most resorts, from having to compete with cheap and predictably sunny foreign holidays. It received a major boost in 1984 with the building of the International Conference Centre, aimed at putting the town on the conference map to rival Birmingham, Harrogate and Brighton. The development spawned a rich market in training and language courses, attracting a financial services industry.

In the 1990s Bournemouth decisively changed its image when it deliberately set out to embrace youth on the back of its large student population. A liberal approach to licensing and a benign attitude to clubs earned the town the nickname (to Brighton's annoyance) of 'party capital of the south'.

The council washes the pavements in the town centre every day of the year, cares lovingly for its 2,000 acres of open space, and ensures that the beaches and the seawater are clean. The town was declared 'Resort of the Year' in 2000.

Above: Bournemouth beach and pier from the east cliff.

Page 112: Blackpool Tower.

Page 113: The Victorian port at Plymouth.

PORTSMOUTH

This is a town with enviable assets: history in abundance, a travel time of only an hour to London, an extensive and beautiful harbour, a naval base and a flourishing passenger ferry trade. It has benefited greatly from Heritage and Millennium funding, and in *HMS Victory* it boasts one of the country's most enduring and best-loved historic monuments, but – paradoxically given all these advantages – the resort is not flourishing, and visitors are falling year on year. The town has suffered from being over-reliant on its past. The Navy is less popular than before, and the historic dockyard is full of (mainly) 'boys' toys'. The waterfront is dislocated from the centre and lacks the youth attraction of its counterparts in Bournemouth or Brighton, for visitors as well as investors. To fulfil its potential the town now needs a broader base of appeal and a clearer strategy.

The beach and pier at Portsmouth. Despite its resources, the resort is punching below its weight.

PLYMOUTH

Plymouth has a similar long history to Portsmouth as a historic naval port, but it has fared even less well. The town suffered heavily from bomb damage in the second world war, but the town failed to use the opportunity to rebuild with either aesthetic or commercial vision.

Plymouth was further severely hit when Devonport dockyard reduced its employees in the early 1980s from 20,000 to 4,000. The town has suffered from inept and indecisive political leadership, which for parochial reasons sacrificed the chance of winning a £30 million lottery bid. A new council is

The lure of the sea – but Plymouth is fading.

trying to regenerate the Victorian Tinside port and bring in new investment, but this may be too little, too late.

BLACKPOOL

Like Brighton, Blackpool was a small fishing community which began to attract visitors from the 1720s and 1730s. By 1780, the emerging resort boasted four substantial hotels, although at the beginning of the nineteenth century its resident population stood at only 500.

Blackpool took off as a seaside resort with the coming of the railway in the 1840s, and proved itself the ideal holiday resort for inhabitants from towns and cities in the northwest of England. Like Brighton, its principal sites are mostly nineteenth century. It boasts the most celebrated landmark of any British seaside resort – Blackpool Tower (1894), modelled on the Eiffel Tower. Like Vancouver (and Liverpool) it has a Stanley Park (1926), but unlike other British resorts it boasts three piers (1863, 1868 and 1894), a giant wheel in the Winter Gardens (1896), the Grand Theatre (1894) and the Pleasure Beach (1905), – now the most visited tourist attraction in Britain, with

over seven million visitors each year. Blackpool's famous illuminations (*above*) were first created in 1912-1913, modelled on Kaiser Wilhelm II's jubilee celebrations in Berlin, allowing the holiday season to extend by eight weeks longer than its rivals.

Blackpool adjusted to the competition from foreign holidays better than many British resorts. In 1975 it became linked to the national motorway network, a major boon. It developed sophisticated corporate facilities, promoted 'mini-breaks', became a centre for high profile events including the World Ballroom Dancing Competition, enhanced its tourist attractions and developed major indoor facilities, such as the Sandcastle and Sea Life Centre. As a result it has become Europe's top seaside resort, with about 10.5 million visitors a year.

It is now attempting to develop itself as the national centre for gambling – Britain's answer to Las Vegas or Atlantic City. Blackpool recognises that to prosper in the new century it has to find a way of becoming internationally competitive.

HULL

Although it is not a seaside resort, Hull is included here because of its initiatives: it easily eclipses all seaside towns in Britain for the grandeur of its vision, and its hunger to advance. A large, essentially Victorian town, it suffered from the familiar story of a decline in local employment – in this case principally fishing and manufacturing. The situation was not all bleak, however. The town benefited hugely in 1981 from the Humber Bridge, which sped up its road communications, and from the Thatcher privatisations of the 1980s, which gave the town a new lease of life and money to spend.

In the mid–1990s a body was established, with wide support across the city, to shape Hull's future. It was to become a pioneering city, its core values being discovery, innovation and leadership. It needed a new visitor attraction, an overhaul of its transport system and the introduction of richer creative and cultural facilities.

Little time was wasted translating these ideas into reality. The major attraction was 'The Deep' (*below*), a £40 million ocean discovery centre at the confluence of the Rivers Hull and Humber, which opened in 2002. A new swing bridge was built to link it with the historic Old Town and the embryonic creative industries quarter. The St Stephen's Project, designed by Norman Foster, is a 28-acre development, improving the image and substance of the town's transport at a cost of some £150 million. The dominant feature will be a 'floating sail' roof bridging the main public boulevard, providing new leisure and retail facilities and a home for the renowned Hull Truck Theatre Company. Among the other initiatives are a £43 million community sports stadium with conference facilities, the £48 million development of Island Wharf and a campus for the universities of Lincolnshire and Humberside.

Good communications have been central to Hull's vision. More than £50 million is being spent on access, while landscaping is being enhanced and imaginative street lighting is being used to create a 'corridor of light'. The city is benefiting from strong and decisive leadership, and is also outward looking, as seen in its formal links with no fewer than six international cities.

In contrast, Brighton and Hove have eschewed the opportunity of being linked with any city abroad. That alone says much. Imagine, too, what Brighton and Hove could achieve with such investment, especially if government put as much money into the south as it does into the north.

The Deep is one of several imaginative projects designed to promote the rejuvenation of Hull.

6
SEASIDE CITIES WORLDWIDE

Inspiration needs also to come from abroad, where seaside resorts have, unsurprisingly, experienced similar challenges as regards transport, fluctuating tourist appeal, weather, a semi–circular shape, vulnerability to military attack and separation from the capital city.

All the cities described briefly here have something to offer Brighton and Hove. The energy and imagination recently shown by Dieppe (*facing page*) shames not only Brighton but many other British towns, too. Vancouver has taken care to retain its historic quarter while developing ultra-modern structures nearby. Seattle has created a dashing seafront, modern attractions inland and an integrated rapid transport system. Marseilles has sunk part of its main road underground. Bilbao has boosted its international stature and its tourism with the Guggenheim Museum (*above*). Barcelona is bursting with energy from every orifice, galvanised by its successful hosting of international events. Cape Town has developed a beautiful waterfront.

Dieppe

Our consideration of seaside resorts abroad begins with that 'dear little place, Dieppe', as Noel Coward patronised it. Dieppe has been chosen because it contrasts so starkly with the depressed and depressing Newhaven at the other end of the Channel crossing. Dieppe has considerable advantages over its British neighbour, being the regional market and shopping centre, whereas Newhaven suffers from being in Brighton's shadow. But Dieppe has also enjoyed imaginative leadership and a large level of public and European Union investment which has resulted in the attractive, thriving port of today. Newhaven, even with its advantages (rail, road, beautiful harbour) has made little of itself. Few Britons can but be embarrassed by it: who doesn't wince at the contrast for visitors disembarking from France!

Dieppe was established as a harbour in the medieval period, and by the sixteenth century it was the principal port in France. Sailors set out from here to discover New York City and Quebec. It was from Dieppe that the French fleet sailed to set fire to Brighton in 1525. Two centuries later Dieppe pioneered the development of the seaside holiday town, as did Brighton. Sea–bathing and promenading burgeoned further in Dieppe in the nineteenth century, stimulated in particular by the railway. In the twentieth century the advent of paid holidays by the French government stimulated tourism in Dieppe, although it then suffered from competition from closely situated resorts like Deauville, and warmer French resorts on the Atlantic coast and Mediterranean.

Dieppe has punched back in the last 15 years with striking success. The town centre has been attractively pedestrianised, the old quarter has been renovated, new green spaces have been created (making a dozen open gardens in all), a rapid bus service has been introduced, the seafront has been given amenities and beautified with new planting, the Cultural Centre has been developed and a new *Cité de la Mer* museum created. If all this can be achieved in a town with a population of just 36,000, imagine what Newhaven (let alone Brighton) should be able to do.

Rejuvenated Dieppe. The town has a small population but an abundance of drive and imagination.

Vancouver

People have lived around Vancouver for more than 10,000 years. Europeans explored the area from the late eighteenth century, and Captain George Vancouver, the Bristol explorer, began to chart it in 1792. The Hudson's Bay Company set up fur-trading posts from 1824, and in 1858 the area was established as a British colony. Change followed swiftly. In 1866, the two colonies of Vancouver Island and British Columbia merged, and they joined the newly established Canadian Federation in 1871. The arrival of the Canadian Pacific Railway in 1886 was the driving economic force of the period, and it shaped much of the city as it is today.

The opening of the Pacific Canal in 1914 stimulated Vancouver's port, as Canadian grain could now be loaded on to ships in the harbour for a much quicker route to European markets. In 1921, the Pacific Highway down to Seattle and Southern California further stimulated trade, and by 1929 the population had grown to 80,000.

The 1930s depression hit Vancouver hard, and it was not until the post-war era that the

city fully found itself again. Hosting the British Empire Games in 1954 helped put it on the map, especially as this was the first sports event to be broadcast live across northern America. Expo 86 provided an even greater boost to the city in 1986, attracting 21 million visitors, and establishing its reputation as an international city. Expo 86 also spawned many developments, including the waterfront, Canada Place (with its tent–sail motif providing a home to the World Trade Centre), hotels, shops and a cruise ship terminal. The Sky Train rapid transit system came at the same time. Asian migration boosted the population in the 1990s, and by 2001 it stood at about 550,000.

Barcelona

The population of Barcelona is four times that of Brighton, and it is also the capital of the rich and powerful region of Catalonia. Its

origins date from the fourth century BC, but not until 988 did it become the capital of an independent state, and until the late fifteenth century it was the seat of the Aragon monarchy. The town grew rapidly during the eighteenth century, and was further boosted in 1888 and 1929 by major international exhibitions.

The Franco period (1936-1975) was sluggish for Barcelona, but after the dictator's death the city took off. The 1922 Olympic Games gave an extraordinary boost to its standing and to its prosperity. By the end of the century it had established an enviable reputation as one of Europe's most progressive cities, renowned for its culture and architecture, as well as for its seafront and its beaches.

A key to Barcelona's success has been a widespread local involvement in the town's success. This is a city that bristles with self-confidence and pride.

SEATTLE

Formed by settlers as a town in 1869, Seattle is situated just over 100 miles south of the Canadian border. A meagre trading, timber and fishing port in its early years, it took off in the late nineteenth century, spurred by the coming of the railway in 1893 and the gold rush from 1897.

In the twentieth century Seattle rapidly developed as a banking centre and was boosted by the demand for ships and aircraft during both world wars. Since 1945 the city's economy has been boosted by tourism, drawn to Seattle's natural beauty, and by high technology companies: Microsoft and Amazon are two of Seattle's biggest firms, as was Boeing until it announced in 2001 that it was moving to Chicago.

Like Brighton, Seattle is constrained by the sea on one side and mountains (the Downs in Brighton's case) on the other. At 560,000, Seattle's population is just about double Brighton's, and the city is inevitably far more affluent. But it also has much to teach Brighton. Its public transport is impeccable,

with a rapid monorail (*top corner of page*) which was built in 1962 for the world fair and is integrated with an efficient bus and tram network. Seattle has been far more successful than Brighton in attracting business, so vital for its financial health. It has a vibrancy and youthfulness which is redolent of Brighton, it manages to cope with its indifferent weather and it maintains its vitality throughout the year. The similarities between the two are, in fact, far stronger than their differences.

Left: The natural beauty of Seattle's setting is a lure for tourists.

Below: The city's skyline includes its famous 'space needle'. Many high-tech firms are based in Seattle.

BILBAO

More than any other city in this brief survey, this was an industrial town, burgeoning rapidly in the nineteenth century. It tried with some success to transform itself into a city based on high-quality service industries. Nothing, however, has shaped the city's outlook as effectively as the opening of the Guggenheim art gallery on the waterfront (*right*) at the end of the twentieth century.

CAPE TOWN

Possibly the oldest inhabited area of the seven cities discussed here, the Cape was not 'discovered' by Europeans until 1488. The European presence was only transitory until the Dutch East India Company established a permanent post at Table Mountain (*left*) in 1652. In 1814, the colony was formally ceded by the Dutch to the British, under whom the city developed rapidly in the nineteenth and early twentieth century.

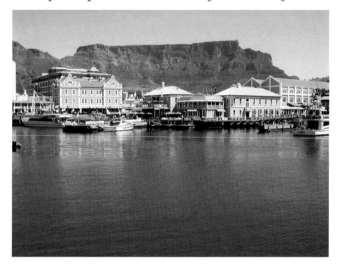

South Africa's economy suffered after it left the Commonwealth and adopted apartheid policies from the 1960s. The coming of multi-national South Africa in the 1990s caused economic turmoil, but it also fully reconnected the country to the international community.

Nothing is more instructive than the Victoria and Albert scheme, showing that waterfront developments can be aesthetically attractive as well as commercially successful.

MARSEILLES

With a population of more than 900,000, Marseilles is over three times the size of Brighton and Hove. With Roman ancestry, a Mediterranean climate and a major port, comparisons with Brighton and Hove might seem superficial. Three facets of Marseilles, however, are instructive. It has built a modern port, giving a massive boost to the town's economy; its coast road has in part been submerged underground; and it displays great style and panache – using and celebrating its water far better than Brighton.

7
WHAT MAKES SEASIDE CITIES SUCCESSFUL

Images of run-down seaside towns, with weather-beaten and unloved seafronts, are some of the most depressing one can encounter. Urban decay always saps the morale, but at seaside towns it is somehow even worse because it appears counter-intuitive: one expects the sea to be life-giving and to impart vitality, to stir the imagination and to lift our eyes beyond the parochial.

Why have some seaside cities been successful? Why have others, with similar advantages and problems, fallen into decay? The successful resorts discussed in the two preceding chapters display common characteristics. All of them have exhibited a sense of purposefulness. All have been imaginative and bold. They have been outward-looking, not insular. They have evaded the death knell of the typical resort cycle: development, popularity, decline, decay.

Successful seaside cities have also benefited from sustained tourist trade, a vital local economy, efficient transport to and within their boundaries, a clean environment, the exploiting of all opportunities for investment and, often, major international events or attractions.

BRIGHTON AND HOVE'S MAJOR STRENGTHS

- Wonderful late eighteenth and nineteenth century buildings, including the (soon to be restored) West Pier and the Palace Pier.
- The two universities – both are growing in strength and also working together as never before, notably with the medical school. The Sussex Innovation Centre is helping link the universities to private enterprise applications.
- Proximity to London – no other northern European country has such a prominent seaside town so close to the capital.
- Growth. The area saw the quickest expansion in the south-east region during 1995-2001, and is expected to keep ahead.
- Quick trains to the capital (49 minutes to Victoria; 51 minutes to London Bridge) with some 15,000 commuters to London each day.
- Brighton Festival, together with cultural profile and exhibition/performance spaces.
- Road links with the M23, and the A27 dual carriageway around the city.
- The financial services sector (notably Amex, Family Assurance).
- Cultural identity, history and resources.
- The sea and the Downs, giving the city its unique quality of life.
- The rapid growth of the multi-media industry (e.g. 'Victoria Real', 'EPIC', 'Get Frank').
- Shoreham harbour and airport, both with considerable untapped potential.
- High numbers of ICT-literate and highly qualified graduates in the city.
- Proximity to Gatwick Airport, the region's principal engine of economic advance.
- A newly unified local authority willing to work with the private sector.
- Sport, being home to Brighton and Hove Albion, Sussex County Cricket Club and the Brighton Bears basketball team.
- An excellent local newspaper, the *Argus*, and magazine, *Brighton & Hove Life* (but no Brighton & Hove television station).
- Conference facilities, albeit ageing and inadequate in size.
- Tourism – on the increase again after years of stagnation.
- A liberal, tolerant and young culture.

Three of the city's great advantages.

Top, elegant architecture: Brunswick Square.

Centre, the universities: Basil Spence buildings at the University of Sussex.

Bottom, rapid communications: the lamented Brighton Belle approaching Patcham.

BRIGHTON AND HOVE'S MAJOR WEAKNESSES

- Shortage of space for new building, and shortage of housing of all kinds, especially affordable housing.
- Transport. The city's roads become easily clogged at pressure times, especially in holiday periods, and there are poor east–west transport links across the region.
- Drab, under-loved parks, and a lack of plants and trees in the city in general.
- A lack of sports fields, and disunity in certain sports – notably rugby – even after the unification of Brighton and Hove.
- The pebbly, steeply sloping beach, unfriendly for swimming.
- A thinly populated and economically poor hinterland: the city's population numbers 260,000, whereas the figure for East Sussex overall is only 758,000.
- Widespread hardship – an April 2002 report (by the Brighton and Hove Regeneration Project) highlighted 'high levels of illiteracy, homelessness, crime and poverty, with 20,000 people unable to read'
- Low-levels of well paid jobs (especially skilled / semi-skilled), and unsatisfactory job retention.
- A failure to attract heritage tourists on a par with York, Bath and Oxford.
- A chronic lack of work ethic among certain groups in the city, although aggregate unemployment has fallen from 12 per cent to less than 4 per cent since 1990.
- Political structures in the city that have not been delivering decisive, strong leadership. The local bureaucracy, and a plethora of bodies and agencies, can be cumbersome, making the decision process too protracted.
- A lack of a strong base in manufacturing industry, and a presence of big firms (other than Amex, which employs 3,000 people) or corporate headquarters.
- A lack of office space or industrial property currently in the city.
- A lingering image as a dirty, dangerous and dingy town. Many still see it as 'scruffy'.
- Heavy dependence on public sector employment which does not create wealth.

- Unpredictable weather, even at the height of summer.
- Education – despite a generally good state education system, fewer than 20 per cent of 16-year-olds are currently achieving 5 GCSE passes, and 200 are leaving school each year with no exam passes to their name.
- Dependence on external support. The city has attracted more than £100m for urban regeneration since 1995, but this will soon dry up. A new dynamism is needed.

A lack of aesthetic sense. The siting of the barrack-style Conference Centre next to the beauty of the Grand Hotel (right) and the sheer ugliness of the King Alfred Centre (below) exemplify urban planning at its very worst.

THE PRINCIPAL OPPORTUNITIES

- Build an international airport.
- Transform Shoreham Harbour.
- Build an international art gallery.
- Develop a rapid transport system.
- Speedily build a major new stadium of high quality for Brighton & Hove Albion.
- Build a new railway station on the outskirts of Brighton.
- Entice international companies into the city.
- Solve the housing shortage.
- Beautify the green areas.
- Construct a contemporary art gallery.
- Establish new museums.
- Clear cars off the seafront.
- Develop the newly-created pedestrianised area.
- Develop a conference centre.
- Build a large spa.
- Use the beach more fully.

THE PRINCIPAL THREATS TO THE CITY

- National Park status and pressure from the green lobby could prevent land being used for industrial and housing development.
- National or regional recession.
- Meltdown in the ICT industry.
- Rising sea levels from global warming.

- A reputation for dirtiness, drugs and dinginess, deterring tourists and trade.
- Political in-fighting or inertia that stunts progress.
- Further terrorist attacks on the scale of September 11, 2001, damaging air travel and economic growth.

Above: The Dome Theatre has been refurbished, and Brighton Museum transformed into a showcase befitting the early 21st century, but the city needs an art gallery of international calibre.

Top right: These sinister-looking, dilapidated buildings off London Road are far from uncommon, giving the city an offputting reputation for dirt and dinginess.

THE SEVEN VIRTUES AND TOMORROW'S CITY

Charles Landry, in his powerful book *The Creative City* (2000), outlined seven areas where innovation and creativity are required to build tomorrow's successful, enduring cities:
- They must be ethical and value-driven communities.
- They should enjoy improved governance and quality of democracy.
- Cities should be environmentally conscious.
- They should acknowledge and celebrate multi-culturalism.
- All parties within the city should become 'stake-holders'.
- History should be treasured and should be combined harmoniously with the new.
- Cities of the future must be 'learning cities'.

THE WAY AHEAD: THE MANIFESTO

The English Tourism Council produced a report in 2001 entitled 'Sea Changes. Creating world-class resorts in England', which criticised the country's seaside resorts for, until recently, exhibiting 'no awareness of the need to change' in the face of challenge from seaside destinations abroad and in inland Britain. Time was not on the resorts' side: 'procrastination and continued inactivity will mean the demise of almost all resorts as they currently stand'. .

Brighton and Hove has been experiencing its City Era since the mid–1980s, but the pace must be accelerated urgently. The proposals outlined in the next chapter will retain (and entrench) the best of the old; will build on the city's strengths; and will have the three 'Cs' as its guiding principles – *culture* (in the broadest sense) because it is one of the city's strengths; *community*, because it must be the city's inhabitants who benefit, not only the visitors; and *commerce*, because the town has been held back in the past by an inadequate economic base and now needs a very strong local economy – not just for employment but to fund the vast sums that must be spent in the coming years.

'Rain at Brighton' by Adrian Hill. The south coast's poor weather has been the city's constant bane.

8
BIRTH OF THE INTERNATIONAL CITY

Brighton and Hove is uniquely placed among seaside towns in Britain and northern Europe to become a major international city. This is its birthright. The ninth era will be the logical conclusion of its long history.

The city's all-important proximity to the capital and to Gatwick airport, its position on the south coast and its dominance in the south-east region give it advantages enjoyed by no other seaside city in northern Europe. If Brighton and Hove became an international city it would benefit not only the city itself (as new jobs and opportunities flooded in, enriching the lives of all its varied inhabitants), but it would give a powerful engine-driving development to the region as a whole.

Britain has London, Edinburgh, Glasgow and Manchester – cities of international renown – but it has no international city by the sea to compare with Nice, Barcelona, Bilbao, Cape Town or Seattle. The English Tourism Council's report 'Sea Changes' counsels urgent action if the country is to have world-class resorts. Brighton and Hove is uniquely placed not only to become Britain's first world-class resort: it must become a true international city in every sense.

Facing page: design by AROS

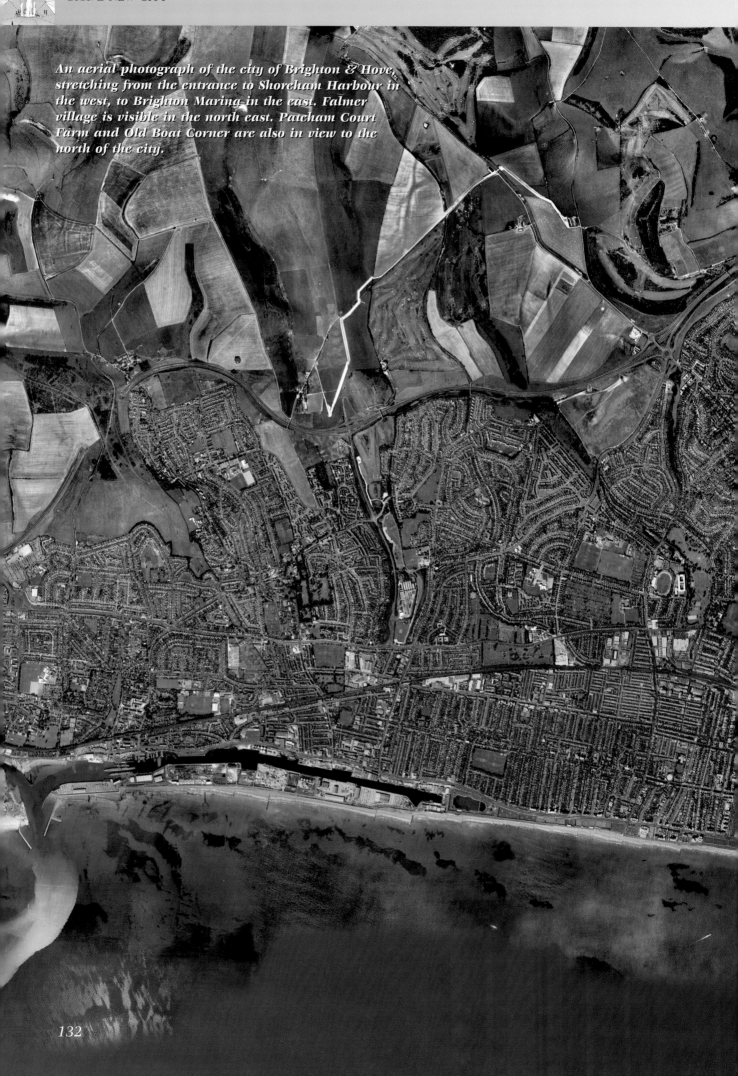

An aerial photograph of the city of Brighton & Hove, stretching from the entrance to Shoreham Harbour in the west, to Brighton Marina in the east. Falmer village is visible in the north east. Patcham Court Farm and Old Boat Corner are also in view to the north of the city.

BRIGHTON INTERNATIONAL STADIUM

5

BRIGHTON PARKWAY

6

NEW RTS SYSTEM

4

HIGH TOWERS IN THE CENTRAL BUSINESS DISTRICT

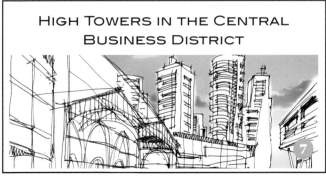
7

HOVE PAVILION

3

SHOREHAM WATERFRONT

2

BRIGHTON INTERNATIONAL AIRPORT

1

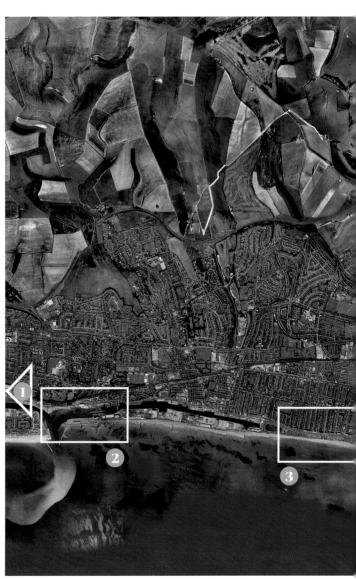

TEN THOUSAND NEW HOMES

CONTEMPORARY ART GALLERIES

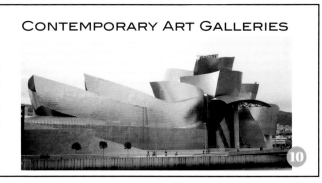

BEAUTIFUL PARKLAND

THREE NEW MUSEUMS

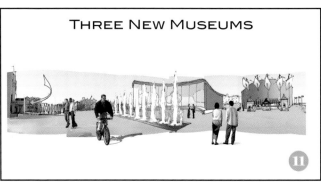

PEDESTRIANISED SEAFRONT

NEW CONFERENCE CENTRE

NEW MARINA ENTRANCE/SPA

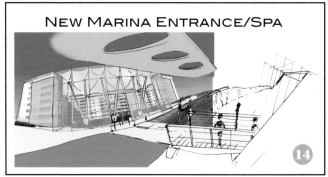

A view of the future with the South Downs in the background.

BRIGHTON INTERNATIONAL AIRPORT

'Brighton International' should be developed on the site of the current Shoreham airport. Excellent road and rail links are ready available. Brighton International will relieve pressure on Gatwick and Heathrow, and cut journeys up to London's airports for those living along the South Coast. Brighton International will help put the city on the international map, and will give a powerful boost to tourism and commerce.

Flights would land and take off over the sea, thus limiting noise pollution.

Shoreham Waterfront

This prime seaside site, which would be linked to central Brighton by the Rapid Transport System (RTS), is ripe for development. The area to the east of the harbour entrance can become a major watersports centre, with rowing, sailing and windsurfing as particular specialities. All these sports will become major growth activities in the next fifty years and would hugely enhance the leisure opportunities of those in the city and beyond.

The long narrow area between the inland water and the sea should be developed for housing, both upmarket and social: few if any development sites in Britain boast a more attractive double aspect view over sea and harbour. Offices and shops should also be built, with a road link to the A27.

The whole east Shoreham Harbour area has been an eyesore for many years, but its potential is enormous. The RTS would allow waterfront commuters to be in central London within an hour. Commuting would be as quick as from Sutton, Ealing or Mill Hill, and the quality of life would be much more pleasant.

Left: *One design for the new Hove Pavilion. Like its elder brother in Brighton, it would occupy a prime spot in the heart of the city – in this case, on Hove Lawns*

HOVE PAVILION

Brighton Pavilion is one of the most famous buildings and landmarks in Britain, and rightly so. Why not build the Hove Pavilion, inspired by inverting the designs of the Brighton Pavilion: that is, Chinese on the outside, with Indian interiors?

No bolder or more profound statement could be made linking both halves of the city. The building must have great panache and presence – a worthy partner to the Brighton Pavilion, of the same stature as the Guggenheim in Bilbao, eclipsing in grandeur and scale the new Turner Gallery in Margate or the Baltic at Gateshead. The Hove Pavilion should house international art of the highest quality, with the Tate providing much of the collection. The Hove Pavilion would help to underline and boost the city's international links, specifically with China and India, whose peoples have made such an important contribution to the city over the years.

THE CITY'S RAPID TRANSPORT SYSTEM

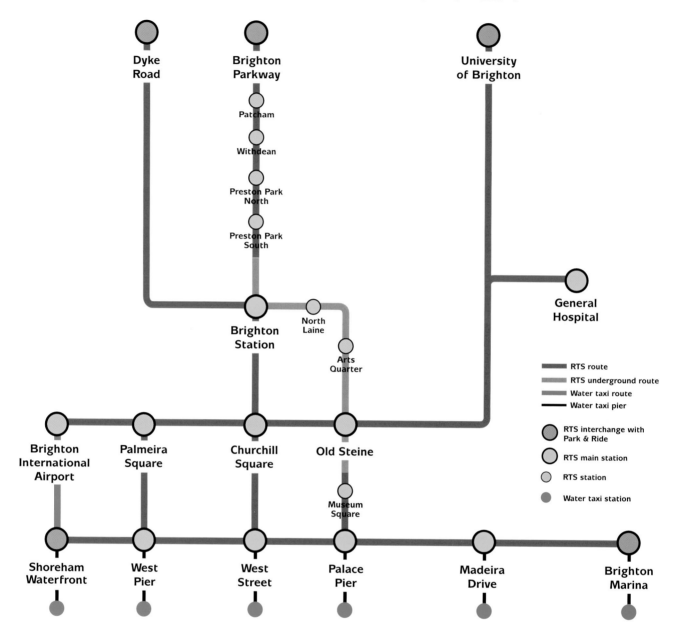

Diagram by Alan Wares

The city badly needs a Rapid Transport System (RTS). A May 2002 report by the South Coast Multi-Modal Group commented that 'over the next 15 to 30 years, current conditions on the corridor's transport networks are likely to significantly worsen if nothing is done'. Other reports highlight the city's chronic traffic congestion as a serious inhibitor of growth (SEEDA 2002).

Solutions are at hand. Cars should be parked in five park-and-rides, one at the top of Dyke Road (1,000 spaces) for those coming in from the west; one at Waterhall (5,000 spaces) near the junction of the A23 and A27 for those coming from the north; one at

Falmer (1,000 spaces) for drivers from the east; and two more at Shoreham Harbour (1,000 spaces) and the Marina (2,000 spaces) for those approaching along the coast roads.

The Dyke Road and Falmer connections would be by bus. Those using the Waterhall, Shoreham Harbour and Marina park-and-rides would mount the RTS's special trams. The tram journey from Waterhall would be along the railway line (with stops at Patcham, Withdean and Preston Park North and South). Three hundred metres before the main Brighton Station the trams would branch off and descend underground (as was first suggested 100 years ago).

Brighton International Stadium and Brighton Parkway

Most now agree (very late in the day) that the city needs a major stadium; not least to house Brighton & Hove Albion, which lost its Goldstone Ground in the 1990s (*see p. 13*). The stadium should be built not at Falmer, but on the playing fields just to the east of the A23 where it meets the A27, and it should eventually seat no fewer than 40,000. The city, and the region, badly needs such a stadium. Road and rail links are ideal. The World Cup has shown how stadiums can be erected in within the space of two to three years. The stadium would be primarily for football, but it would also host other sporting as well as cultural events.

A new railway station, 'Brighton Parkway', would be built by the park-and-ride at Waterhall, adjacent to Brighton International

The World Cup stadium at Saitama, Japan, prvides an ideal greenfiled model for an international stadium

Stadium. All trains would stop there (instead of at Preston Park). Those wanting to ride on the RTS or use the stadium would alight at Parkway. The new station would cut traffic: commuters to London would use it, rather than battling though the central Brighton traffic to access the mainline station.

Right: The RTS – trams and coaches – can be powered by renewable sources, including recycled fuel.

The first underground stop would be 'Brighton Station', with an underground walkway of 400 metres connecting to it the main station concourse, then 'North Laine' and 'Arts Quarter' and 'Old Steine' before emerging into the open on 'Museum Square', the new pedestrianised concourse in front of the Palace Pier. The trams would run on rails on the road, going to the Marina in the east and Brighton International in the west. The RTS would run off recycled fuel and would thus be environmentally friendly

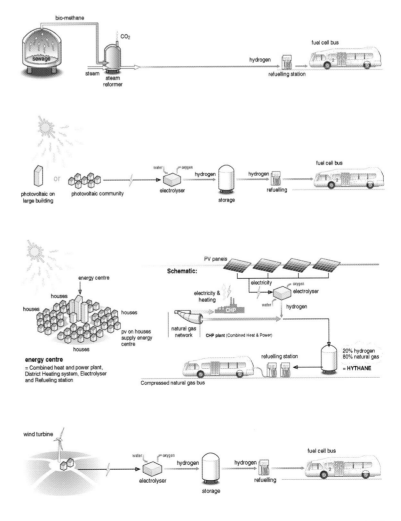

High Towers in the Central Business District

As the front cover of this book shows, a series of towers is advocated for the 'central business district'. The envisaged high-view gallery/restaurant would give the city a landmark to rival the Blackpool Tower or the London Eye.

Five skyscrapers should be erected by 2020. At least two of them would be for businesses: many international companies would want to set up their UK offices here, close to Gatwick and Brighton International Airports. Two towers would be for flats, and one would be for a hotel. The new companies which would flood into the city and its towers would bring serious, much needed money to the local economy, allowing the city's coffers to swell.

Skyscrapers are growing rapidly across the country: London has 422, with a further 22 under construction, while Birmingham has 28 and is building six. In contrast, Frankfurt has 240 skyscrapers while Toronto (third behind New York and Chicago) has 1060 . No one could accuse Brighton and Hove, with these five proposed new towers, of hubris.

The city's present high-rise buildings (the Hilton West Pier, Sussex Heights and the council flats) have been lambasted in this book not because they are tall but because they are ugly. Towers can be, and must be, objects of beauty. Set back from the seafront, they would not be visible when looking along it – in contrast with the high-rises of today.

The proposal is not as monstrous as some will think: Hugh Casson was an early advocate of skyscrapers for Brighton. Their advent would allow many more buildings to be preserved rather than knocked down, as would inevitably be the case eventually in order to meet changing needs.

TEN THOUSAND NEW HOMES

Affordable housing needs to be built, both houses and flats. The Shoreham Harbour development would provide homes for many. Other houses must come on greenfield sites within the A27 'beltway'. The bullet must be bitten. The green lobby and the South Downs National Park must not be allowed to stand in the way. Open space between Ditchling Road and the Lewes Road would provide a suitable site for extensive new building. New playing fields should also be created as part of this widescale development. Building outside the A27 beltway should be forbidden: inside, everywhere between Lancing and the Lewes Road should be open for development to meet current and future needs.

The open space currently making up Hollingbury Park and the Hollingbury golf links between Lewes Road to the south-east and Ditchling Road to the north-west.

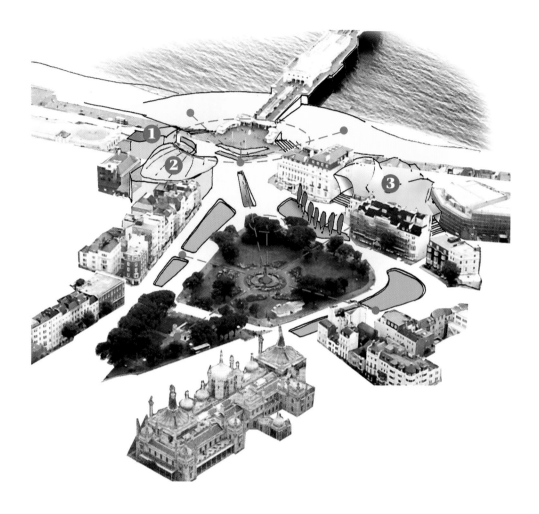

The pedestrianisation of the Old Steine and the seafront would allow easy access to the three new museums.

1. The Museum of the Sea

2. The Science Museum

3. The Museum of Film and Performance

The three museums together would make the new 'Museum Square'. Traffic would be re-directed on to fee-paying roads underground.

THREE NEW MUSEUMS

The Cultural Quarter which at present consists of the Pavilion, Dome, the refurbished Brighton Museum and the new library, should be enhanced not just by the proposed Contemporary Art Gallery, but also by three proposed museums situated in the newly pedestrianised area where the Steine meets the sea.

One would be a science museum, an offshoot from the Science Museum in Kensington; the second would be a Museum of Film and Performance, fed in part from the Museum of the Moving Image, including an IMAX Cinema and recognising the seminal place of the city in the early history of film; and the third would be a Museum of the Sea, incorporating the current Sea Life Museum and celebrating the city's history as a fishing town and a pioneering spa resort. 'Museum Square' would become a place of delight, rather than the traffic-dominated, nondescript area it is today.

Beautiful Parkland

Brighton and Hove's parks and green spaces are often disappointing. There far are too few trees, flowers, hanging plants and colour. This can be improved by a determined policy of planting and care. One park should be dedicated as a botanical garden, with large greenhouses, a Kew-by-the-sea. The gardens leading down to the Brighton Pavilion and the Brighton Pier (the Level, Victoria Gardens and the Steine) are bitty. They should be joined together, and the roads which transect these gardens should be put underground. An unbroken green park nearly a mile long would thus be created, and it could be planted with beautiful plants and trees, as could the many other parks in the city. Some derelict or green areas should be turned into playing fields.

Contemporary Art Gallery

The Hove Pavilion would be the major international gallery, but the city also needs a contemporary art gallery, more avant-garde, in the heart of the Cultural Quarter. A ready site is available – in the derelict buildings facing the Royal Pavilion, where Edward Street meets the Steine. The building itself should be of scintillating design, while also aligning itself with the prevailing skyline of the Steine's Regency buildings.

PEDESTRIANISED SEAFRONT (KING'S ROAD)

The whole seafront? Ideally yes, but in practical terms it would be the kilometre stretch from Museum Square to just west of the West Pier. The road itself, or parts of it, would be put underground, as in Marseilles.

The cost could be met by tolls. Fifty thousand cars currently use Kings Road daily. To charge them £2 for using the underpass would raise £36 million a year. The area above, with attractive trees and flowers, would become a prime seaside site for leisure development. The long, broad expanse would again be safe for promenading, for eating and drinking, for listening to live music and for enjoying the fresh sea air.

The RTS tram would run on tracks through the pedestrianised area. Another gain would be that it would tidy up the point where West Street (leading down from the station) meets the sea, turning the most disappointing and depressing place in the entire city into a place of beauty.

Right: An imaginary picture, painted by Victoria Jones OB, of how the main seafront area might look once it was pedestrianised. The Grand Hotel and the buildings to the east of Kingswest would be preserved as they are, but the Conference Centre and Kingswest would be replaced.

Top: The Palace Pier roundabout as it is today – marred by traffic and very unfriendly to pedestrians. Note the vile, tall building at the start of Marine Parade, which, like Embassy Court, assaults the panorama and is profoundly out of place.

Bottom: An AROS design for how the area could look with the three museums, and without the cars. Note the integration of the RTS sytstem.

NEW CONFERENCE CENTRE

Would anyone mourn the destruction of the Kingswest Odeon or the Conference Centre? The cinema could go underground – cinemas are one activity which do not in fact benefit from light (or, amazingly, from sea views). The Conference Centre could then occupy the entire site. The building must be one of real flair and interest – as in the design envisaged here. What a super prize for a world-class architect!

Spa/New Marina Entrance

The entrance to the city from the east is marred by the ugly Marine Gate and the orange Courcelles building with Sussex Heights and the Hilton West Pier looming in the distance above them. The Marina entrance is quite spectacularly unattractive by any standards. The car park beneath the cliffs is unsightly and sullies the view of the Marina as a whole. The solution is simple – design a new entrance to the Marina leading down from Wilson Avenue (obliterating the gasometers in the process).

Marine Gate could be wrapped up to disguise it or, more charitably, a sympathetic building could be erected to its immediate east in order to mask it. The area around Black Rock could also be cleaned up, with the

RTS coming along Madeira Drive and then on into the Marina.

The English Tourism Council in a 2002 report said: 'Seaside resorts have perhaps the biggest asset of all, and should exploit the natural health links with the sea: thalassotherapy, mineral baths, hydro-centres, day spas with crêche facilities, outdoor "sea air" watersports.' The report exhorts local authorities to seize this opportunity. What more needs to be said?

A multi-faceted spa should be built over the large car park under the cliffs, catering for a wide range of health tourists and a wide range of budgets. This development would allow the city to once more become a spa resort, as it was in the eighteenth century.

The huge ASDA car park is not only ugly but an inefficient use of space. It could be covered by an elegant new structure which would contain Britain's largest and most diverse health spa, with direct access from both the cliff top and the Marina, as shown in pink (right).

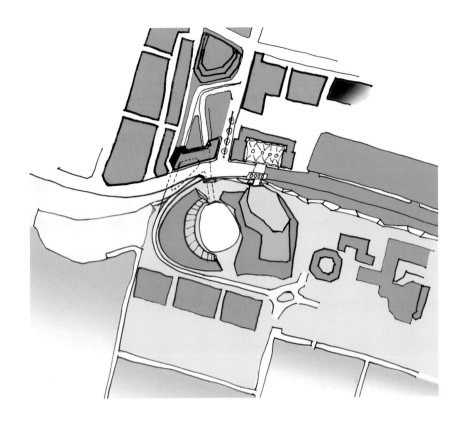

A More Active Beach and Promenade Area

The beach is little used for most of the year. It should have areas designed to suit all different age groups and interests. The area just off the shingle should be developed to include a whole range of free facilities for the young to enjoy, including skateboard and skating parks. There needs to be much more in the city for the young to enjoy without having to spend money.

The city should be ashamed of how little it has offered young people in the past. This is now beginning to change, and not before time. Busy young people are generally well-behaved young people.

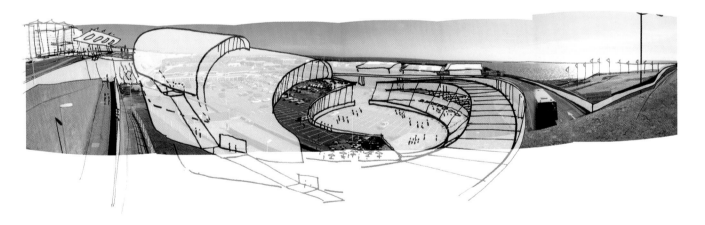

FIFTEEN FURTHER IDEAS

- Twin Brighton and Hove with exciting seaside cities abroad. (Rejecting this option, as in the past, vividly illustrates the city's insularity.)

- Stage a major international event in the city – European City of Culture in 2008 would be such an event – to give it a once-in-the-arm injection. If the bid fails, go for another event.

- Give the Brighton Festival the funding it deserves. England's biggest arts festival needs to have a much higher profile and to be much better supported.

- Devise an annual event for the city, akin to the Cannes Film Festival or the Frankfurt Book Fair, which will raise its international standing. An annual media/creative/ICT/sporting/environmental/spiritual festival might fit the bill.

- Institute an elected mayor to give the city real drive and dynamism and to break out of the stasis of political in-fighting endemic in the current structure. An elected mayor will be an important stepping stone to building a more participatory democracy in the city. Brighton and Hove should become a model for democratic cities of the future.

- Give every local area a fixed sum for beautification, to be spent how each community decides. Reward with extra cash those localities who use the money to best effect.

- Knock down Embassy Court, Hilton West Pier and other excrescences along the seafront and inside the city. Hold a series of parties to celebrate. Majorca provides an example of determined local action to demolish its bad buildings – a number of disastrous developments, including awful hotels, have been demolished, and appropriate structures put in their place. We should not be afraid of following suit.

- Join Brighton and Hove rugby clubs together to create a serious force, similar to those clubs which give the city a national profile in football, cricket, basketball and hockey. Sport matters.

- Appoint a figure with vision (e.g. architects Norman Foster or Richard Rogers) to come in immediately to sort out once and for all the protracted wrangle over the West Pier.

- Clean the streets in the centre every night, and ensure that the beaches are cleaner and better maintained. Erect new street lights wherever the designs of current lights jar, ideally wall-mounted and always in keeping with the area.

- Establish a local television company exclusively covering the city and its immediate environment.

- Re-house sections of Peacehaven and Telscombe Cliffs (buying up properties as they go on to the market over a 60-year span and giving very generous compensation). Then grass over the areas to give some unbroken acreage of green Downs and sea views (and a nature reserve) between Saltdean and Newhaven, in place of the endless ribbon development.

- Build a Cornish-style harbour at Rottingdean. It would re-juvenate the village and would provide an attractive destination for leisure craft on a coast short of harbours.

- Establish immediately the old rectangular town as an area which is sacrosanct. Recover, where possible, the old town's original features, and define a heritage trail linking it with more recent developments. The city needs to tell its story much more clearly than it does at present.

- Establish the city as a thug-free zone.

Bibliography

Adland, David *Brighton Music Halls*, Baron Birch for Quotes Ltd, 1994

Beevers, David *Brighton Revealed*, Brighton Pavilion Art Gallery & Museum 1995

Betjeman, John *Victorian and Edwardian Brighton from Old Photographs*, Batsford, 1972

Bramwell, David *Cheeky Guide to Brighton*, Cheeky Chops Publications, 2001

Carder, Timothy *The Encyclopaedia of Brighton*, East Sussex County Library 1990

Chapman, Brigid *Brighton in the 50s*, Lewes Book Guild, 1996

Clunn, Harold *Capital-by-the-sea*, Southern Publishing Co, 1953

Collins, Joyce, *Dr Brighton's Indian Patients*, Brighton Books Publishing, 1997

Dale, Antony *Brighton Old and New*, EP Publishing, 1976

Dale, Antony *Brighton Town and Brighton People*, Phillimore, 1976

Dale, Antony *Theatre Royal Brighton*, Oriel Press, 1980

Dale, Antony *Fashionable Brighton 1820–1860*, Oriel Press 1967

Davies, Peter *Historic Brighton and Hove*, 1982

Elleray, Robert *Brighton: a Pictorial History*, Phillimore, 1987

Farrant, Sue *The Growth of Brighton and Hove 1840–1939*, University of Sussex Centre for Continuing Education, 1980

Farrant, Sue *A Guide to the Buildings of Brighton*, McMillan Martin

Gilbert, Edmund *Brighton: Old Ocean's Bauble*, Flare Books, 1975

Gray, Frank *Hove Pioneers of the Arrival of Film*, University of Brighton Press, 1996

Gray, Fred *Walking on Water: a West Pier Story*, the Brighton West Pier Trust, 1998

Gray, James *Brighton Between the Wars*, Batsford, 1976

Hall, Peter *Cities in Civilisation*, Orion, 1999

Hollingdale, Eileen *Brighton in Retrospect*, Kensington Press, 1974

Horlock Chris *Brighton: A Century in Photographs*, SB Publications 2001

Horlock, Chris *Brighton & Hove Then & Now* (2 volumes), SB Publications, 1999/2000

Landry, Charles *The Creative City*, Earthsea Publications, 2001

Lockhart, Ann *Brighton and Hove*, Pitkin Guides, 1997

Middleton, Judy *Brighton and Hove in Old Photographs* (two volumes) 1988/1994

Montgomery, John *Brighton Past and Present*, Countryside Books, 1986

Morley, John *The Making of the Royal Pavilion*, Philip Wilson Publishing

Musgrave, Clifford *A Pictorial History of Brighton and the Royal Pavilion,* Pitkin Pictures, 1971

Musgrave, Clifford *Life in Brighton*, Archon Books, 1970

Owen, Patricia *The Development of Brighton as a Resort Town*; Royal Pavilion, Art Gallery & Museum, 1996

Ravetz, Joe *City-region 2020*, Earthsea Publications, 2000

Richardson, Nigel *Breakfast in Brighton*, Gollancz, 1998

Rogers, Richard *Cities for a Small Country*, Faber & Faber, 2000

Rykwert, Joseph *The Seduction of Place*, Weidenfield & Nicolson, 2000

Sampson, Mark *Brighton History and Guide*, Alan Sutton, 1994

Smith, Gilly *Juicy Guide to Brighton*, Juicy, 2001

Trimingham, Adam *Trimingham's Brighton*, Pomegranate Press, 1999

Turner, John *London, Brighton and South Coast Railway*, London, Batsford, 1977

Underwood, Eric *Brighton*, Batsford 1997

Brighton, a Different Kind of City, Brighton City Council 2001

Brighton and Hove Visitor Guide, Benn & Cronin

Brighton Behind the Front, QueenSpark Books 1990

Brighton Festival Programmes 1982–1984, Newman Thompson Ltd

Kiss and Kill, Royal Pavilion, 2002

Locum Destinations seminar, 2002

Sea Changes English Tourism Council, 2001

Acknowledgements

This book, more than many, has benefited from wisdom and advice from those far more knowledgeable than the author. I have been bowled over by the generosity in both time and experience of so many people who were also willing to fit in with the absurd time-frame (three months) that I had set myself for researching and writing the book.

The following kindly agreed to be interviewed: Steve Bassam, Sue Berry, Mick Dunford, Roger French, Simon Fanshawe, Gavin Henderson, Glynn Jones, Geoff Lockwood, Simon Smith and Adam Trimingham. Several of the above also kindly agreed to read sections of the book, or the entire manuscript.

At the Council the following were particularly helpful: Lucas Eliot, Justine Halpine, Jamie Healy, Mel Sensicle, Amanda Sheppard. At the museum I would particularly like to thank David Beevers and Stella Beddoe, who went out of their way to be exceptionally helpful. I would also like to thank John Roles who, despite the extra strain of opening the museum, provided wise counsel, and all the staff at the Local Studies Library in Brighton, who were particularly helpful to me.

Many people provided photographs: Chris Horlock has been quite outstandingly supportive and helpful throughout. A celebrated author on Brighton, and the possessor of an unrivalled collection of archive photographs, he was patient, enthusiastic and tactful, despite knowing infinitely more about the subject than I. His photographs are extensively used throughout. Fred Gray provided helpful advice and photos on the West Pier, and Frank Gray advice on films featuring Brighton. Henry Smith was exceptionally generous with his own fine collection of slides. Victoria Parr at the Argus was very helpful with pictures. Victoria Jones (ex-Brighton College) painted the design on the inside back cover.

The following helped in a variety of different ways and I would like to thank them collectively: Nick Beeby of English Heritage, Richard Brightwell, Ken Bodfish, Simon Bradshaw, Jo Crockett, John Davies, Ian Duncan, Robert Griffiths, Louise James of Canford, Michael Hooker, Kim Lancaster, Miriam Jones, Brian Moore, Murray at 'Mint', Stephen Neiman, Stewart Newton, Chris and Sue Nurse, Jean Pappworth of Walberswick, Peter Rutter, Alasdair Smith, Gilly Smith, Dr. Helen Walker, Wendy Walker, Ian Waring and Sir David Watson.

My co-convenor of the Brighton and Hove City Forum, Douglas Mckittrick, has been a most jocular and stimulating companion for the nearly five years we have lived in Brighton. I have learned a great deal from him, and from all the forum speakers and participants at this most thought-provoking body. I would like to thank two outstanding historians of the town, both now deceased: Antony Dale (OB) and Clifford Musgrave. I would also like to thank Tim Carder (OB) who wrote The Encyclopaedia of Brighton.

At Brighton College I would like to thank in particular Mary-Anne Brightwell, Mary-Ann Collins, Adrian and Anne Corder, Victoria McDonagh, Ken Grocott, Angie Moore, Joanne Riley, Philip Robinson, Joanna Seldon, Jessica Seldon, Juliet Smith, Simon Smith, Paul Thomas, Anthony Whitestone and Jeff Wood. Sir Lindsay Bryson was responsible for our being in Brighton by rashly appointing me headmaster of Brighton College. The pupils have been endlessly delightful and stimulating, and I would particularly like to thank those on the upper sixth reading party to Exmoor in April who appeared interested in their headmaster writing this book in their midst. Edward Twohig, director of art at Brighton College, took the new photographs, showing tremendous flair and patience at the very worst time of the academic year for any director of art.

The visualisations in chapter eight and the cover were designed by the pioneering international architects AROS, based in London. I would particularly like to thank Nick Readett-Bayley, Chris Cotton, Mark Limbrick, Mark Gleghorn, Sara-Jane Allen, Whitby and Bird (engineers). I would also like to thank James Alexander of Locum Destinations for his ideas and for putting me onto AROS. At Medialab in Brighton, who produce *Brighton and Hove Life*, I would like to thank Leonard Stall and Alan Wares for all their technical support and work: Alan's enthusiasm and skill were crucial. Michael Chowen, chairman of British Bookshops, helped make publication possible by guaranteeing to purchase a number of copies. My thanks also to Sonia Land, my agent, for not minding my writing this book.

I would finally like thank two people who have helped throughout the entire project. Matthew Nurse, who left Brighton College in July 2001, has been research assistant from day one and has been a model of resourcefulness, energy, rigour and diplomacy. He will surely have a glowing future ahead of him. Finally, David Arscott of Pomegranate Press has been the ideal publisher for any author. He reminded me of editors that there used to be in the best publishing houses when they employed people of erudition and imagination before the businessmen took over.

Anthony Seldon

Picture credits

The author and publishers wish to thank the following for permission to use their illustrations in the book.

Argus: pages 63(top),65(middle),93,95(top),105,106(top two)

AROS: cover graphics and Chapter 8 concepts
Further Chapter 8 images by Getmapping (base satellite imagery) and Whitby Bird & Partners Engineers (rapid transit system)

Belmontpress: frontispiece, title page,29,31,58–59,67(bottom),68(bottom),89,92

Sue Berry: various

Birmingham Museum & Art Gallery: page 52

Board of Tourism, Bournemouth: page 114

Peter Booth: pages 24(middle),66(bottom)

Brighton & Hove City Council: pages 110–111

Brighton Pavilion, Art Gallery & Museums: pages 39,42,49(bottom),74–75,76,84(bottom),100,101,129

Canal + Images: page 102

Department of Tourism, Blackpool: pages 112,116

Department of Tourism, Hull: pages 113,117

Department of Tourism, Portsmouth: page 115

Dieppe Tourist Office: pages 118,120

Fred Gray: pages 56,57,69(top)

Guggenheim Museum, Bilbao: pages 119, 123(top)

Gavin Henderson: pages 61(top),105(bottom)

Chris Horlock: pages 11,12(bottom),13(middle),15(bottom),16(both),17(bottom),18,20(both), 21(bottom two),22(both),23,24(bottom),25(top)26(both),28(bottom),33(bottom),36,37(bottom),46(top),50, 53(bottom)54,60,62,63(bottom),65(bottom),66(top),72,73(both),77,83,84(top),90–91,106(bottom),109(top), 126(bottom)

Howlett Clarke Cushman solicitors, Brighton: page 47

Robert Jeeves: page 13(bottom)

Lufthanza: page 136

Plymouth Marketing Bureau: page 115

Edward Twohig:pages 10,12(top),13(top),14(top),15(top),17(top),19(both),21(toptwo),24(top), 25(bottom)27, 28(top),33(top),34,35(both),37(top),44,45,48,55,64,65(top),67(top),68(top),69(bottom);70,71,78,79,80,81,81,85,86, 88,94(top),95(bottom),96,97,98,99,104(top),107,108,109(bottom),124,126(top two),127,128

Science & Society Library, London: pages 6,53(top),103(top)

Henry Smith: pages 40,46(bottom),51

Spanish Embassy Picture Gallery, London: page 121(bottom)

Tate Gallery, London: page 49(top)

Washington State Tourism Department, London: pages 121(top),122

Philip Wilson Publications: page 41

Index

Page numbers in **bold** refer to illustrations

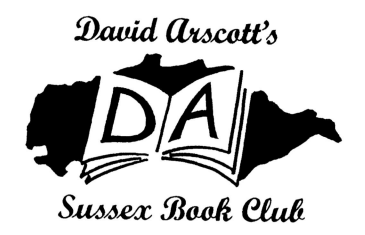

David Arscott's

Sussex Book Club

The home of books about Sussex

So many books are written about Sussex that it's difficult to keep track of them all. But no longer! Writer/publisher David Arscott has founded a lively book club which will keep you abreast of everything that's being written and which gives you the opportunity to select from a wide range of new titles.

This is a rare no-catches book club:

- Membership is completely free
- There's no obligation to buy
- You won't be sent books you haven't asked for
- Any books you order will be sent to you free of post & packing
- Your details will not be passed on to any other organisation

To enrol in this growing fraternity of Sussex book lovers simply send your name and address to:

The Sussex Book Club
Dolphin House
51 St Nicholas Lane
Lewes, Sussex BN7 2JZ

or email:
sussexbooks@aol.com